# Progressive Web Apps with React

Create lightning fast web apps with native power using React and Firebase

**Scott Domes**

BIRMINGHAM - MUMBAI

# Progressive Web Apps with React

First published: October 2017

Production reference: 1181017

Published by Packt Publishing Ltd.
Livery Place
35 Livery Street
Birmingham
B3 2PB, UK.
ISBN 978-1-78829-755-4

www.packtpub.com

# Credits

**Author**
Scott Domes

**Reviewer**
Amar Gharat

**Commissioning Editor**
Kunal Chaudhari

**Acquisition Editor**
Shweta Pant

**Content Development Editor**
Onkar Wani

**Technical Editor**
Akhil Nair

**Copy Editor**
Shaila Kusanale

**Project Coordinator**
Devanshi Doshi

**Proofreader**
Safis Editing

**Indexer**
Tejal Daruwale Soni

**Graphics**
Jason Monteiro

**Production Coordinator**
Melwyn Dsa

# About the Author

**Scott Domes** is a full stack developer who specializes in React, with a passion for building powerful and performant web applications, and for playing with shiny new technologies. Based out of Vancouver, when not coding he's probably out hiking some mountain, or getting lost in a good book. Scott loves to teach and talk about web development, and is always looking to learn new things.

*A special thank you to Packt Publishing for giving me the chance to write this book, and for Onkar and Shweta for assisting me on this journey. Check out https://www.packtpub.com/ for an excellent selection of quality programming books.*

*Thank you to my technical readers: Warren Vosper, Mario Grasso, Andrew Hayter, and Miodrag Vujkovic. A special thanks to everyone at MuseFind for their support and feedback, and to my family and friends for their encouragement.*

*Lastly, thanks to you, the reader, for picking up this book. I hope you enjoy it. You can follow me on Twitter and Medium as @scottdomes, or my website, scottdomes.com*

# About the Reviewer

**Amar Gharat** focuses on developing creative and unique web applications using LAMP, open source, and cutting-edge technology as well as delivering work on time to meet the deadlines with dedicated team work.

He has a total work experience of 11 years, and has executed projects from design, development, production, and support. He defines requirements and plans project life cycle deployment.

He also has knowledge of SDLC and process models, and defines resources and schedules for project implementation. He plans and schedules project deliverables, goals, milestones, and tracking them to closure.

Strong leadership and people management are Amar's core skills.

He develops and delivers progress reports, proposals, requirements documentation, and presentations; submits status reports from the project team, analyzes results, and troubleshoots problem areas; manages changes in project scope, identifies potential crises, and devises contingency plans.

He defines project success criteria and disseminates them to involved parties throughout the project life cycle, and helps build, develop, and grow any business relationships vital to the success of the project.

Research, innovate, propose, and discuss product area improvements is what he believes in, and he works on clear requirements with business managers and product managers. He gets projects developed using agile, and is responsible for code reviews, documentation, and maintenance of applications. He's also responsible for core product metrics and end-to-end responsibility for programming of new pages/microsites.

He develops internal web-based interfaces, and provides technical leadership to team members. He's known for delivering time-based task assignments, and is an expert in unit testing.

Amar is also experienced in portal management.

# www.PacktPub.com

For support files and downloads related to your book, please visit `www.PacktPub.com`. Did you know that Packt offers eBook versions of every book published, with PDF and ePub files available? You can upgrade to the eBook version at `www.PacktPub.com` and as a print book customer, you are entitled to a discount on the eBook copy. Get in touch with us at `service@packtpub.com` for more details.

At `www.PacktPub.com`, you can also read a collection of free technical articles, sign up for a range of free newsletters and receive exclusive discounts and offers on Packt books and eBooks.

`https://www.packtpub.com/mapt`

Get the most in-demand software skills with Mapt. Mapt gives you full access to all Packt books and video courses, as well as industry-leading tools to help you plan your personal development and advance your career.

## Why subscribe?

- Fully searchable across every book published by Packt
- Copy and paste, print, and bookmark content
- On demand and accessible via a web browser

# Customer Feedback

Thanks for purchasing this Packt book. At Packt, quality is at the heart of our editorial process. To help us improve, please leave us an honest review on this book's Amazon page at https://www.amazon.com/dp/1788297555. If you'd like to join our team of regular reviewers, you can email us at customerreviews@packtpub.com. We award our regular reviewers with free eBooks and videos in exchange for their valuable feedback. Help us be relentless in improving our products!

# Table of Contents

# Preface

Progressive Web Apps with React aims to give you everything you need to know about the future of web development. **Progressive Web Apps** (**PWAs**) are becoming more and more common for companies looking to leverage the best the web can offer, powered by cutting-edge technologies that bridge the gap between web apps and native apps.

In this book, we'll leverage the power of the popular JavaScript library React.js to create a fast and functional UI. Then, we'll add Progressive Web App features such as push notifications and instant loading, using revolutionary new web technology. Finally, we'll streamline our app's performance and look at how to best measure its speed.

By the end of this book, you will feel comfortable with both React and PWAs, and be ready for the future of the web.

# What this book covers

Chapter 1, *Creating Our App Structure*, gives a brief overview of what exactly you will be learning to build-- a real-time chat application with push notifications and offline support. You will get to learn about the challenges that such an app presents, and get a brief overview of the technologies that will be discussed in this book. By the end of the chapter, you will set up the application structure of a chat app, with HTML and CSS.

Chapter 2, *Getting Started with Webpack*, says that before you write any React code, you need to set up the webpack build process. In this chapter, you will be introduced to webpack; you will learn to install the package and set up some basic configuration as well as get the development server running. This chapter will get you ready to jump into React.

Chapter 3, *Our App's Login Page*, introduces you to React time! In this chapter, you will learn to write the first two components: an App wrapper to contain the application and a LoginContainer. Learn about rendering with ReactDOM and JSX, and write a basic form to allow the users to log in. By the end of this chapter, you will be familiar and comfortable with the React syntax.

Chapter 4, *Easy Backend Setup With Firebase*, informs that the login form looks great, but is lacking actual functionality. To move forward, you will need a backend database and authentication solution to communicate with it. This chapter will introduce you to Firebase by Google. Set up the application on the Firebase console, and then program the login and signup functionality for the form.

Chapter 5, *Routing with React*, lets you know that once the user logs in, you want to redirect them to the main chat view. Therefore, in this chapter, you will learn to build that main view and then set up the React Router that allows the users to move between the pages. Lastly, learn to add a third view the individual user view--and explore parameter matching in URLs.

Chapter 6, *Completing Our App*, takes you through the last step in building the basic application, adding functionality to the chat and user views. You will learn to write and read data from Firebase, taking advantage of React life cycle methods to do so. Once that's done, your web application will be complete, but it's not quite progressive yet!

Chapter 7, *Adding a Service Worker*, covers service workers and how they work. Here, you'll understand how to register a custom service worker and learn about its life cycle, and then hook into the default Firebase messaging service worker.

Chapter 8, *Using a Service Worker to Send Push Notifications*, teaches you to configure the app now that our service worker is ready, to be able to send the push notifications. You will use Firebase Cloud Messaging to manage sending these notifications, and add customization to control how and when they are sent on desktop and mobile.

Chapter 9, *Making Our App Installable with a Manifest*, teaches that a manifest is a JSON file that allows users to save your app to their home screen. You will learn to create the manifest and understand the best practices as well as iOS-specific considerations. You will also learn to customize your splash screen and icons.

Chapter 10, *The App Shell*, puts across the point of the App Shell pattern being a key concept in PWAs, but what advantages does it bring? You will be introduced to both the shell and the RAIL system of progressive enhancement, and then move some of you app's layout out of React for optimal rendering.

Chapter 11, *Chunking JavaScript to Optimize Performance with Webpack*, explores the PRPL pattern, its goals and methods, as well as an overview of how to achieve it in your app. Then, you will dive in, splitting up the JavaScript into chunks based on routes, and then lazy loading the secondary routes.

Chapter 12, *Ready to Cache*, walks through how you can leverage the service worker to achieve offline capability, by understanding the new Cache API, and how to use it with your service worker to cache the JavaScript chunks.

Chapter 13, *Auditing Our App*, says it's now time to check our work! In this chapter, you will be introduced to Lighthouse and understand how to audit PWAs with Lighthouse.

Chapter 14, *Conclusion and Next Steps*, Your first PWA is complete! In the development process, you built most of the PWA infrastructure manually. In this chapter, you will get to learn about the helper libraries and shortcuts to save time, and you'll also explore the future of PWA development. Additionally, you will come across suggestions about the future project ideas and improvements that can be made to your chat app, as an extra challenge.

# What you need for this book

All you require is a computer that can run Node.js (https://nodejs.org/en/download/), a text editor for writing code, and the latest version of the Chrome browser. If you want to test your application on mobile, you'll also need an Android or iOS phone.

# Who this book is for

This book is for JavaScript developers who want to develop high-performance Web User interfaces. This book requires basic knowledge of HTML, CSS and JavaScript.

# Conventions

In this book, you will find a number of text styles that distinguish between different kinds of information. Here are some examples of these styles and an explanation of their meaning. Code words in text, database table names, folder names, filenames, file extensions, pathnames, dummy URLs, user input, and Twitter handles are shown as follows: Inside App.js, we first import the LoginContainer.

A block of code is set as follows:

```
import React, { Component } from 'react';
import LoginContainer from './LoginContainer';
import './app.css';


class App extends Component {
  render() {
    return <LoginContainer />
  }
}

export default App;
```

When we wish to draw your attention to a particular part of a code block, the relevant lines or items are set in bold:

```
if (module.hot) {
  module.hot.accept('./components/App', () => {
    const NextApp = require('./components/App').default;
    ReactDOM.render(
      <App/>,
      document.getElementById('root')
    );
  });
}
```

Any command-line input or output is written as follows:

```
yarn add css-loader style-loader
```

**New terms** and **important words** are shown in bold. Words that you see on the screen, for example, in menus or dialog boxes, appear in the text like this: Flip back to the app, and you should see the **Hello from LoginContainer** of our new component.

Warnings or important notes appear like this.

Tips and tricks appear like this.

# Reader feedback

Feedback from our readers is always welcome. Let us know what you think about this book-what you liked or disliked. Reader feedback is important for us as it helps us develop titles that you will really get the most out of. To send us general feedback, simply email feedback@packtpub.com, and mention the book's title in the subject of your message. If there is a topic that you have expertise in and you are interested in either writing or contributing to a book, see our author guide at www.packtpub.com/authors.

# Customer support

Now that you are the proud owner of a Packt book, we have a number of things to help you to get the most from your purchase.

# Downloading the example code

You can download the example code files for this book from your account at http://www.packtpub.com. If you purchased this book elsewhere, you can visit http://www.packtpub.com/support and register to have the files emailed directly to you. You can download the code files by following these steps:

1. Log in or register to our website using your email address and password.
2. Hover the mouse pointer on the **SUPPORT** tab at the top.
3. Click on **Code Downloads & Errata**.
4. Enter the name of the book in the **Search** box.
5. Select the book for which you're looking to download the code files.
6. Choose from the drop-down menu where you purchased this book from.
7. Click on **Code Download**.

Once the file is downloaded, please make sure that you unzip or extract the folder using the latest version of:

- WinRAR / 7-Zip for Windows
- Zipeg / iZip / UnRarX for Mac
- 7-Zip / PeaZip for Linux

The code bundle for the book is also hosted on GitHub at https://github.com/PacktPublishing/Progressive-Web-Apps-with-React. We also have other code bundles from our rich catalog of books and videos available at https://github.com/PacktPublishing/. Check them out!

# Errata

Although we have taken every care to ensure the accuracy of our content, mistakes do happen. If you find a mistake in one of our books-maybe a mistake in the text or the code-we would be grateful if you could report this to us. By doing so, you can save other readers from frustration and help us improve subsequent versions of this book. If you find any errata, please report them by visiting http://www.packtpub.com/submit-errata, selecting your book, clicking on the **Errata Submission Form** link, and entering the details of your errata. Once your errata are verified, your submission will be accepted and the errata will be uploaded to our website or added to any list of existing errata under the Errata section of that title. To view the previously submitted errata, go to https://www.packtpub.com/books/content/support and enter the name of the book in the search field. The required information will appear under the **Errata** section.

# Piracy

Piracy of copyrighted material on the internet is an ongoing problem across all media. At Packt, we take the protection of our copyright and licenses very seriously. If you come across any illegal copies of our works in any form on the internet, please provide us with the location address or website name immediately so that we can pursue a remedy. Please contact us at copyright@packtpub.com with a link to the suspected pirated material. We appreciate your help in protecting our authors and our ability to bring you valuable content.

# Questions

If you have a problem with any aspect of this book, you can contact us at questions@packtpub.com, and we will do our best to address the problem.

# 1
# Creating Our App Structure

Welcome to *Progressive Web Apps with React*!

This book will take you through the entire process of building a React application that also functions as a Progressive Web App. We'll cover not only the "how" of constructing such an application, but also highlight best practices and how to measure your application to ensure successful implementation of PWA features.

Progressive Web Apps are poised to become the future of web applications. They promise a bevy of additional functionality, such as push notifications and the ability to be installed, which pushes them into the realm of native iOS or Android apps. Additionally, a strong focus on performance (taking advantage of cutting-edge web technology) means that PWAs create apps that are fast for everyone.

We'll cover each facet of PWAs in depth, as well as the process of converting a regular web application into a progressive one. We'll also dive deep into React best practices, using libraries such as React Router.

To check your code for this and future chapters, you can view the completed project at `https://github.com/scottdomes/chatastrophe/`. The repository includes branches for each chapter. Visit `https://github.com/scottdomes/chatastrophe/tree/chapter1` for this chapter's final code.

In this chapter, we will get started with the basic structure of our application. Here's what we'll cover:

- The use cases of Progressive Web Apps
- The basic user stories we want our app to fulfill
- The project structure and basic HTML
- Installing dependencies
- Getting started with React

First, let's set the scene for our application's journey.

# Setting the scene

One of your friends calls you on the phone, bursting with excitement about his latest start-up idea (you know the one). You patiently listen to his description, but respectfully decline to be a part of it. He's disappointed, but understands and promises to keep you updated on the project details. You murmur your assent.

A few months later, he meets you at your work and announces that he has found a group of serious investors, and he needs you to help him build the software he promised them. You again decline, but when discussing compensation, he mentions a number that you can't refuse. A week later, you're on a plane to San Francisco.

In front of the investors (who are, to your surprise, a rapt audience), your friend guides you through the basics of the application. In between the buzzwords ("mass interconnection" and "global community"), you gather just enough to summarize the application in a sentence.

"So, it's a chat room… for everyone in the world… all at once…"

Your friend smiles. "Yes."

You're bewildered by the image of a million strangers all talking at once on the same application, in the same room, but the investors break into applause. As you head for the door, your friend again announces how they'd like to compensate you… citing an even higher number than before. You sit down.

# The problem

"The problem," your friend explains, "is that this chat room has to be for everyone."

"Global community," you say with a knowing nod.

"Exactly. Everyone. Even if they have terrible internet in some hut in the desert. They should be included."

"Mass interconnection," you add.

"Exactly! So it needs to be fast. And lightweight. And beautiful. And dynamic."

"So everyone will be talking at once? Won't that be-"

"A worldwide collective, yes."

## The other problem

"The other problem," your friend declares, "is that our users will mostly be on their phones. On the go."

"So you want to do an iOS and Android app?"

Your friend waves his hand. "No, no. No one downloads apps anymore. Especially in developing countries; that takes too much bandwidth. Remember, worldwide collective."

"So a web app."

"Yes. A web collective."

Despite your best instincts, the project intrigues you. How do you craft a web application to be as fast as possible? How do you make it work under all network conditions? How do you make a chat application with all the conveniences of a native app, but for the web?

You sigh and shake his hand. "Let's get to work."

## Beginning work

Welcome to the world of Progressive Web Applications.

In the preceding scenario, the problems your friend was describing are exactly the problems **PWAs (Progressive Web Applications)** are crafted to solve.

The first problem is that many users will be visiting your web page under poor network conditions. They may be a Silicon Valley technocrat on their iPhone in a coffee shop with bad WiFi, or they may be a Bangladeshi villager in a remote location. Either way, they will not stick around if your site isn't optimized for them, for everyone.

How fast your application loads--its performance--thus becomes an accessibility concern. PWAs solve this by loading quickly the first time, and even more quickly every time after that. We'll talk more about how they do so as the book progresses.

Second, the installation process for mobile apps is an obstacle for users. It means that your users need to be extra committed to engaging with your application--enough to give up storage space and time, and expose themselves to the possibility of malicious and intrusive code, and that's before they even get the chance to try the app!

What if we can provide the native app experience without the initial investment? PWAs are an attempt to bridge that gap. Again, we'll talk in subsequent chapters about how they do so, and how successful they actually are. However, these are both worthy challenges, and solving both will be a huge user experience win for our application.

# Why Progressive Web Apps?

Many static web pages do a fantastic job of performance. However, when all you need to do is render some HTML, CSS, and a smattering of JavaScript, it's less of a struggle to work well under all network conditions.

When we start talking about web applications--large, complex, JavaScript-based workhorses--performance becomes a significant challenge. Our frontend will have a lot of code. Our user needs to download all that code if they want to use our app to its fullest potential. How do we ensure that they're not staring at a blank loading screen for ten seconds, as 500 KB of JavaScript initializes?

Therefore, most of our performance enhancements will center around managing the JavaScript problem. This is especially true with React.

# Why React?

**React** is quickly becoming the go-to solution for frontend web applications. Why? This is because it's fast, elegant, and makes managing large applications easy.

In other words, it makes complexity simple. There's no reason a PWA has to use React, though. PWAs can be any web app or site.

React does have one major benefit--its component pattern, where UIs are split into distinct pieces. As we'll see, the component pattern lets us break our interface into small chunks of code to alleviate the preceding JavaScript downloading issue. However, other than that, any frontend framework will work just as well for a PWA.

The advantage of React is that it is a beautiful and fun way to build frontend applications. It's also an in-demand skill. If you pair knowledge of React with experience with PWAs, you'll be about as future-ready as one can be in the fast-moving web development world.

# A rose by any other name

You tell your friend about your learnings on PWAs and React, but before you finish, he waves his hand and interrupts.

"Yeah, yeah. Hey, what do you think the name should be?"

Once again, you're struck with the unnerving feeling that all of this was a mistake, that you never should have jumped on board this questionable venture, this potential catastrophe.

"Chatastrophe," you blurt out.

Your friend smiles and claps you on the back. "Brilliant. Okay, get Reacting or whatever!"

# User stories

Before we begin building our app, let's take a deeper look at what exactly we want to achieve.

We can start with user stories. A user story is a description of a specific feature of an application, framed from the perspective of one of our users.

Here's the framework, as suggested by *Jon Dobrowolski*:

*Users should be able to _____.*
*As a user, I want to do ___ because ____.*
*Given that I'm doing ___, I should be able to ___ in order to ___.*

Not all features require the whole framework, though. Let's start with some basic examples:

- Users should be able to log in and out of the application

Pretty straightforward. I don't think we need to add the justification for this, as it is a fairly basic feature.

Let's move on to something more advanced:

- Users should be able to view their messages even when offline
- As a user, I want to be able to check my messages without needing an internet connection, because I may need to read them on the go
- Given that I start the application without internet access, I should be able to view all past messages

Let's cover some of the more basic functionality of the app. Users should be able to send and receive messages in real-time.

Real-time functionality will be key to our application. There's no point in having chat unless it's fast and fluid:

- Users should be able to view all messages by a given author
- As a user, I want to be able to view a list of all messages sent by a given user, because I may need to view their contribution to the conversation without the noise of others' messages
- Given that I click on a user's email, I should be taken to a profile view with all their messages

The profile view is a special feature you suggested to the client to manage the inevitable chaos of the main chat room.

Let's add a couple more PWA-specific user stories:

- Users should receive push notifications when a message is sent by another user
- As a user, I want to be constantly updated on the progress of the conversation, because I don't want to miss anything important
- Given that the chat is not open or visible on my screen, I should receive notifications for each message sent by another user

And installing:

- Users should be able to install the app on their mobile device
- As a user, I want to be able to open the application without navigating to the URL in my browser, because I want easy access to the chat room
- Given that I have signed up to the chat for the first time, I should be prompted to install the app on my device

Don't worry about how we will achieve these goals; we'll cover that in due time. For now, let's just continue documenting what we want to do.

Our client was big on performance, so let's specify some performance-specific goals:

- Users should be able to load the app in under 5 seconds, even under shaky network conditions
- As a user, I want to be able to interact with the app as quickly as possible, because I don't want to be stuck waiting for it to load

- Given that I have opened the application using a poor internet connection, I should still have it load in under 5 seconds

Load in under 5 seconds is still a bit vague in terms of what that means for our application. We'll revisit this story in more depth in the chapters on performance.

The previously mentioned user stories cover the basic functionality of our app. Let's talk about the specific challenges these points present.

# Application challenges

With each of the following, I encourage you to think about how you will solve these problems within the context of a web application. Hopefully, this will give you a better insight into what we try to achieve with PWAs, and the difficulties we face.

# Instant loading

With Progressive Web Apps, we aim to provide an experience that is closer to a native app (one downloaded from the Apple App Store, Google Play Store, or another app store) than your typical web application. One of the advantages native apps have, of course, is that all relevant files are predownloaded and installed, while each time a user visits a web application, they may have to download all the assets again.

The solution? When the user first visits the page, download those assets and then save them for later (also known as caching). Then, when the user reopens the application, instead of downloading the files again over the internet (slow), we simply retrieve them from the user's device (fast).

However, this only works for when the user revisits the application. For the initial visit, we still have to download everything. This situation is particularly precarious, because when the user first visits Chatastrophe, they're not yet sold on its value, and so, are likely to leave (for good) if loading takes too long.

We need to ensure that our assets are as optimized as possible, and we download as little as possible on that first visit, so that the user stays around.

In short, fast loading for the first visit, near-instant loading for every subsequent visit.

# Push notifications

There's no point in a chat application without notifications! Again, we're trying to emulate what has traditionally been a native app feature--push notifications directly to the user's device.

This problem is trickier than it might seem. Push notifications are only received when the app isn't open (that's the whole point, after all). So, if our web application isn't open and running, how can we possibly run the code to display a notification?

The answer is to use a third-party service that is engineered to send notifications to registered devices. So, rather than the device receiving the message alerting its user, the device sending the message alerts our notification service, which then notifies all relevant devices.

We also need a piece of code that is constantly "on"--always running and waiting to receive notifications from the third-party service and display them. This challenge only recently became solvable with web technology, and is one of the reasons PWAs are so exciting.

For now, don't worry if this distinction doesn't "click" yet. We'll go into it in greater detail later. For now, the point is that push notifications will be an interesting challenge for our web application.

# Offline access

Even when our user isn't connected to the internet, they should be able to check past messages and navigate around our application.

The answer turns out to go hand-in-hand with the earlier discussion on instant loading. We simply need to cache everything our app needs to function, and then load that on demand; simply, of course, being the operative word.

# Mobile-first design

For years, the big buzzword of web design has been responsive--websites that look just as good when scaled from desktop to mobile size.

PWAs are, in essence, responsive design on steroids, expanding design for mobile to every aspect of the app, from appearance to functionality.

However, at the end of the day, we need to ensure that our app looks great on every screen size. It also needs to look good under the restrictions we've already discussed. We can't rely too much on big background images or intense graphics. We need a simple and good-looking UI, engineered for both looks and performance.

# Progressive enhancement

The bottleneck of performance with any React application is downloading and running the JavaScript. Our entire application code will be contained in JavaScript files--and our app won't work until those are executed. That means our users may be stuck staring at a white screen (with zero functionality) until that JavaScript is ready to go.

**Progressive enhancement** is a technique that aims to fix that problem. In essence, it means that a user's experience should get progressively better as the application downloads, depending on the user's browser. In other words, the application experience improves as time goes on (and more of the application downloads), and as a user's software improves.

A user with the most modern browser, the fastest internet connection, and the application fully downloaded will have the best experience, but a user with an outdated browser, a shaky connection, and who just landed on the page will also have a quality experience.

This means our `React.js` application needs to have some functionality without any JavaScript. This is a fun challenge.

Think of our UX as a series of layers, from good to fantastic, that we build up as time goes on.

# Let's get going

I hope the preceding overview has given you a specific idea of what we're trying to accomplish with this application, and also the roadblocks to achieving those aims. There are a lot of challenges, but as we work through our user stories, we'll deal with them one by one, until we have a fast and functional Progressive Web App.

With the challenges mentioned, you can see the general trend: good performance and user experience under any condition. Certainly a worthy goal, and exactly why PWA techniques are applicable to any web app; they simply promise a better experience for everyone.

Once we start building our application, we'll also see that solving these problems is still a challenge, but all very achievable with React.

The next step is to get everything set up for our application, and create our basic folder structure with HTML and CSS.

# Our app skeleton

First things first. Before we start building our React application, let's get set up with the basic HTML and CSS--the skeleton of our application, if you will, upon which we will heap the React muscles:

1.  Open up your Terminal and switch to whichever directory you want to store your project in.
2.  Then, we'll make our app directory with mkdir chatastrophe. Let's go inside that folder, make another folder within it named public, and within public, touch index.html. If you're on Windows, use type nul > index.html instead of touch:

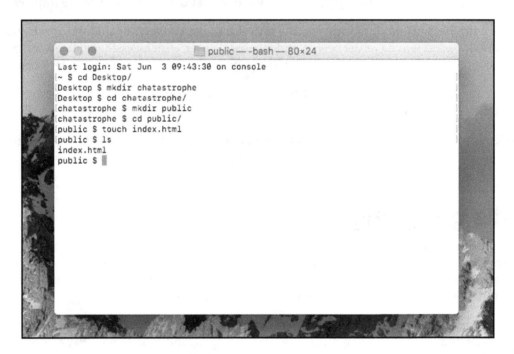

3.  Then, open up the whole chatastrophe folder in your text editor of choice. I'll be using **Sublime Text 3** for this tutorial. Open up the index.html file, and let's write some HTML!

4. Let's start with the basic HTML elements. Create a `<html>` tag, and within that, `<head>` and `<body>`.

5. This wouldn't be a programming tutorial without a hello world, so within the body, let's put `Hello world!` within an `<h1>` tag.

6. Then, open up `index.html` within your browser:

```
1  <html>
2      <head>
3      </head>
4      <body>
5          <h1>Hello world!</h1>
6      </body>
7  </html>
```

Our goal by the end of the chapter is to display the exact same as the preceding illustration, but using React to render our `<h1>`.

Why did we put our `index.html` inside the public folder? Well, our HTML is the first thing our users will download when they hit our page. They will download it exactly as we see it here. This is in sharp contrast to our React JavaScript, which will be transpiled (more on that in the next chapter) before being served to the client. Our React code, as we write it, will be private. Our HTML, as we write it, will be public.

This is a distinction that will make more sense as we move into the React world, but for now, just know that the convention is to put HTML and static assets in the public folder.

# CSS and assets

Our good friend at the start-up (now dubbed Chatastrophe--what have you done?) has tapped a designer to provide some basic assets for us. These include a send icon for our chat box, and a logo for the application. You're not a fan of the style, but *c'est la vie*.

Let's go ahead and download the image files from `https://github.com/scottdomes/chatastrophe-assets`. You can download them by clicking on the **Clone or Download** button, and then selecting **Download as Zip**. Then, unzip those into the `public` folder, in a new folder called `assets` (all asset files should thus be in `chatastrophe/public/assets`).

Before we continue, we can ensure that our assets look okay by testing them in our index.html. Above <h1>, let's put in an img tag, with the src set to /img/logo.png, and an ID as test-image:

```
<img src="assets/icon.png" id="test-image"/>
```

Here's what it should look like:

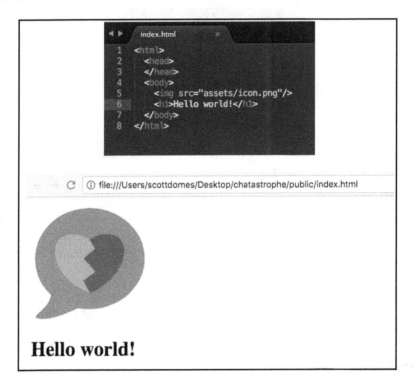

This is even more beautiful.

The last thing we need to do is add our CSS. By the luck of the gods, all of our CSS has been mysteriously prepared for us, saving us the cumbersome task of styling our application. All we have to do is pull in assets/app.css.

We include it in our `index.html` with a link tag:

We should see an immediate change to our page. The background should be a gradiant, and the image should now have a slightly pulsing animation:

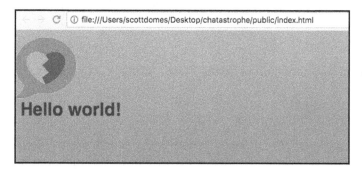

It worked! That does it for our main assets. Let's move on to some improvements to our HTML.

# Meta tags and favicons

Our application will be mobile-first, as we have already discussed. To ensure that our HTML is fully optimized, let's add a bit more markup.

First, let's add a DOCTYPE declaration to the top of `index.html`. This tells the browser what kind of document to expect. In HTML 5 (the newest version of HTML), it always looks like this:

```
<!DOCTYPE html>
```

Next, we need to add a meta tag for `viewport` width. It looks like this:

```
<meta name="viewport" content="width=device-width, initial-scale=1">
```

What does this do? Essentially, it tells the browser to display the web page at the same width as its screen. So, if the web page seems to be 960px and our device is 320px wide, rather than zooming out and showing the whole page, it'll instead squish all the content down until it's 320px.

As you might expect, this is only a good idea if your website is responsive and able to adapt to a smaller size. However, since responsiveness is one of our main goals, let's do this from the start. Add this tag within the `<head>` of our document.

A couple more tags to go! The character set we use on our web page can be encoded in a couple of different ways: **Unicode** and **ISO-8859-1**. You can look up these encodings for more information, but long story short, we're using Unicode. Let's add it like so, right below the previous `<meta>` tag:

```
<meta charset="utf-8">
```

While we're at it, let's add the language the HTML is in. On our existing `<html>` tag, add `lang="en"`:

```
<html lang="en">
```

Okay, that about does it for HTML housekeeping. The last thing we need is a **favicon**, the little icon displayed next to the title in the browser tab. This is included in our assets bundle, so all we have to do is link it up (right underneath our `<meta>` tags):

```
<link rel="shortcut icon" href="assets/favicon.ico" type="image/x-icon">
```

Your browser tab should now look like this:

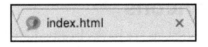

With that, we're done!

Next, we'll look at how we will include React in our project, and all the other dependencies we will need.

# What is npm?

A React application is primarily JavaScript. If you have experience working with JavaScript, you know that the browser is perfectly capable of parsing and executing JavaScript on its own.

In most basic websites, we link to the JavaScript needed for the page in a `<script>` tag, and the browser downloads and runs it.

We'll be doing something similar with our React application (with considerable complications; more on that in `Chapter 2`, *Getting Started with Webpack*).

However, JavaScript is no longer confined to the browser. More and more applications are using JavaScript on the backend as well, with JavaScript running in its own environment.

Long story short, JavaScript is now everywhere, and the driving force behind this proliferation is `Node.js`, a JavaScript runtime library, which lets you run JavaScript outside of a browser environment.

Okay, this is exciting, but why does this matter for our React project?

Node also introduced the idea of packages to JavaScript. Packages are essentially third-party libraries of code that you can install to your application and then import and use where and when you need them. You can use packages even if your application is not a Node application.

React is one such package. Webpack, mentioned earlier, is another one. In short, in order to build a complex web application, we will inevitably rely on a lot of other people's code, so we need packages, and we need **Node's package manager** (shorthand `npm`) to install them.

We'll also use `npm` to start up our application and do some basic tasks, but its primary purpose is to manage packages.

# Node setup

Okay, enough said. Let's go ahead and install Node, which comes bundled with npm:

1. Go to https://nodejs.org and download the latest stable release of Node:

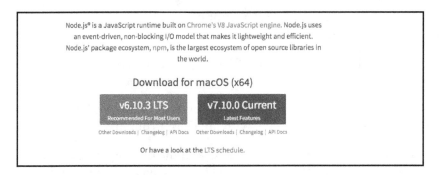

2. Here, I would choose **v6.10.3**, the one recommended for most users.
3. Once that is installed, open up your terminal and run node -v just to confirm the installation:

4. You can also confirm that npm has been included by running npm -v.

Just to reiterate, Node is a JavaScript runtime used to execute JavaScript outside of the browser, and npm is a method of managing modules of JavaScript code. We won't be working with Node directly in this book, but we will be using npm a lot.

# The dark side of npm

In the past year, npm has come under fire for various reasons.

- It can be slow (just try installing large packages over a poor Wi-Fi connection)
- Its installation process can lead to different results for different developers on the same project
- It doesn't work offline, even if you've downloaded the package before

In response to these issues, Facebook came out with a package manager called **Yarn.** Yarn is essentially a wrapper around npm, giving the same basic functionality with an extra layer of goodness. Let's go ahead and install it so that we can use it to manage our packages!

Visit https://yarnpkg.com/en/docs/install for installation instructions. For macOS, note that you'll need **Homebrew** (which is like npm for macOS packages--packages everywhere!), which you can get at https://brew.sh/.

# Project initiation

The next thing we need to do is initiate our application as an npm project. Let's try it out, and then we'll discuss why we needed to do so:

1. Inside your project folder, in your terminal, type yarn init and hit enter.
2. It'll ask you a series of questions. The first one is the most important--the name of our application. It should just take the name of the current folder (chatastrophe). If it doesn't, just enter chatastrophe. From there, just hit enter to skip the rest of the questions, accepting the default answers. These questions would matter more if we were planning on publishing our own package, but we're not, so no worries!
3. If you take a look at your project folder after completing the yarn init, you'll notice that it added a package.json file with our project name and version. Our package.json is important, in that it will act as a list of our dependencies--the package we will install via yarn.

Enough talking about dependencies, though, let's install our first one! What better choice than to install React?

# Installing React

Let's try it by running `yarn add react@15.6.1` from within your `project` folder.

 We're installing a specific version of React (15.6.1) to ensure compatibility with other dependencies, and to ensure that there are no unexpected problems as new versions are released.

Once the installation is complete, you should see React added to our `package.json` under dependencies. You'll also see that `yarn` generated a `node_modules` folder and a `yarn.lock` file.

The `node_modules` folder is where all our packages will live. If you open it up, you can see that there are several folders already. We've not only installed React, but everything that React depends on--dependencies on dependencies.

As you might imagine, the `node_modules` folder can get quite hefty. So, we don't check it into source control. When a new developer joins the team and downloads the project files, they can then install the dependencies independently, based on the `package.json`; this saves time and space.

However, we need to ensure that they get the same packages as everyone else, and the same version; this is where the `yarn.lock` file comes in.

The previously mentioned setup ensures that we are ready to safely use third-party libraries. We have the `package.json`, `yarn.lock`, and `node_modules` folders in our project. Before we continue, let's ensure that adding React worked.

# Using React

Let's confirm that React is in our project by using it to render a simple element to our screen. This will be our first dipping of our feet into React, so go slow and ensure that you understand each step.

First, we need to import our React package (which we just installed with `yarn`) into our `index.html` so that we can use it there.

To do this, we add a `<script>` tag with the path to the main React file within our node-modules folder. This tag looks like this:

```
<script src="../node_modules/react/dist/react.js"></script>
```

Place this in your `index.html`, at the bottom of the `body` tag (before the closing `</body>`).

Okay, we have React! Let's use it to make a simple `<h1>` tag, just like the one we wrote in HTML.

React has a function called `createElement` for this purpose. It takes three arguments: element type, something called props (more on that later), and the children (what goes inside the tag).

For us, it looks like this:

```
React.createElement('h1', null, 'Hello from React!')
```

This function call creates an element that looks as follows:

```
<h1>Hello from React!</h1>
```

To confirm that it will work, let's `console.log` it out:

```
<script src="../node_modules/react/dist/react.js"></script>
<script>
  console.log(React.createElement('h1', null, 'Hello from react!'))
</script>
```

Reload `index.html`, then right-click or control-click and select **Inspect** to open up DevTools in Chrome and switch to the **Console** tab. There, we see our element… or not. Instead of the HTML output, we get something like this:

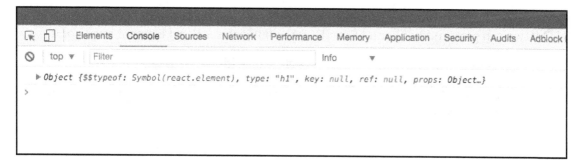

This is not the HTML element we might have expected, but we can see that React has worked in its own way. We have a JavaScript object with a type field of h1. Let's see whether we can transform this into an actual HTML tag on the screen.

# Welcome to ReactDOM

Here's a secret about React--it's a library for creating UIs, but not a library for rendering UIs. In itself, it has no mechanism for rendering a UI to the browser.

Fortunately, the creators of React also have a package called **ReactDOM** for exactly this purpose. Let's install it and then see how it works.

First, we install it with yarn add react-dom@15.6.1.

Then, require it in index.html in much the same way as React:

```
<body>
  <img src="assets/icon.png" id="test-image"/>
  <h1>Hello world!</h1>
  <div id="root"></div>
  <script src="../node_modules/react/dist/react.js"></script>
  <script src="../node_modules/react-dom/dist/react-dom.js"></script>
  <script>
    console.log(React.createElement('h1', null, 'Hello from react!'));
  </script>
</body&gt;
```

ReactDOM has a function called render, which takes two arguments: the React element to be rendered to the screen (hey, we have that already!), and the HTML element it will be rendered inside.

So, we have the first argument, but not the second. We need something in our existing HTML we can grab and hook into; ReactDOM will inject our React element inside of it.

So, below our existing <h1> tag, create an empty div with the ID root.

Then, in our ReactDOM.render function, we'll pass in the React element, and then use document.getElementById to grab our new div.

Here's what our `index.html` should look like:

```html
<!DOCTYPE html>
<html lang="en">
  <head>
    <meta name="viewport" content="width=device-width, initial-scale=1">
    <meta charset="utf-8">
    <link rel="stylesheet" href="assets/app.css">
    <link rel="shortcut icon" href="assets/favicon.ico" type="image/x-
icon">
  </head>
  <body>
    <img src="assets/icon.png" id="test-image"/>
    <h1>Hello world!</h1>
    <div id="root"></div>
    <script src="../node_modules/react/dist/react.js"></script>
    <script src="../node_modules/react-dom/dist/react-dom.js"></script>
    <script>
      ReactDOM.render(React.createElement('h1', null, 'Hello from react!'),
      document.getElementById('root'));
    </script>
  </body>
</html>
```

Reload the page, and you should see `'Hello from React!'` text in the middle of the screen!

# Summary

Success!

We will be diving deeper (much, much deeper) into both ReactDOM and React in the next few chapters. We'll learn how to create elements in a much more intuitive way, and also how React makes building UIs a dream.

For now, we have our project skeleton ready to go—the basis of our future application. Great work!

Our next step is to finish the last stage of preparation, and take a deep look at one of our most important dependencies--a tool called Webpack.

# 2
# Getting Started with Webpack

This chapter is all about Webpack: what it is, how to use it, and why we care. However, before we dive into Webpack, I have a confession to make.

We cheated a bit in the last chapter on application setup. There's one last piece of our folder structure we need to add--the place where our React files will live.

As we discussed in the *Dependencies* section of the last chapter, one of React's killer features is the *componentization of user interfaces*--splitting them up into small chunks of related HTML and JavaScript. For instance, a "Save" button may be one component, sitting inside a form component, next to a Profile Information component, and so on.

The beauty of the component structure is that everything related to a particular piece of the UI sits together (separation of concerns), also, these sections are in brief, readable files. As a developer, you can easily find what you're looking for by navigating the folder structure, rather than scrolling through a monolithic JavaScript file.

In this chapter, we'll cover the following topics:

- How to structure our React project
- Setting up Webpack
- Adding a Dev server
- Getting started with JavaScript transpilation with Babel
- Activating hot reloading
- Building for production

# Our project structure

Let's see what this looks like in practice. In our `chatastrophe` project folder, create an `src` folder (which should be next to the `public` and `node_modules` folder in the root of the project folder).

The `src` folder is where all our React files will live. To illustrate what this will look like, let's create some mock files.

Inside `src`, make another folder, called `components`. Inside that folder, let's make three JavaScript files. You can name them whatever you like, but for example purposes, I'll call them `Component1.js`, `Component2.js`, and `Component3.js`.

Imagine that each of these component files holds a bit of our user interface. We need all three files to construct a complete UI. How do we import them all?

Well, we can do what we've done so far when we needed to use JavaScript files. We can create a `script` tag for each component in our `index.html`. That's the brute force way.

However, as our application grows, this approach will quickly become unwieldy. An application such as Facebook, for example, will have tens of thousands of components. We can't write tens of thousands of `script` tags!

Ideally, we'd have only one `script` tag, with all our JavaScript combined. We need a tool that takes our varied files and squishes them together, giving us the best of both worlds-- organized, separated code for the developer, and compressed, optimized code for the user.

"But wait, Scott," you might say, "if we put all our code in one file, won't that take longer for the browser to download? Isn't it a good thing to have small, separate files?"

You're exactly right. We don't want to go back to a monolithic single file in the end, but neither do we want thousands of separate files. We need a happy medium of a handful of code files, and we'll get to that medium. However, to start, let's see how we can bundle multiple JavaScript files into just one using our new friend--**Webpack**.

# Welcome to Webpack

Our goal for this section is to take the JavaScript sitting in our script tag in our `index.html` (the line responsible for rendering our "Hello from React!") and move that to a JavaScript file in the `src` folder, which is then bundled and injected into the HTML by Webpack.

It sounds complicated, but it's simpler than it sounds, thanks to the magic of Webpack. Let's get started:

1.  First, we need to install Webpack:

    **`yarn add webpack@3.5.4`**

    If you check the `package.json`, you should see Webpack listed under our dependencies. For this book, I'll be using **version 3.5.4**; if you run into any inexplicable problems, try specifying this version with `yarn add webpack@3.5.4`:

2.  Now, we need to tell Webpack what to do. Let's start by moving our React code into the `src` folder. Inside `chatastrophe/src`, create a file called `index.js`.

3.  Then, type in the following code:

    `console.log('hello from index.js!');`

    Our goal is to get this greeting to display in our browser console.

4.  Okay, let's try out Webpack. In your Terminal, type the following:

    **`node_modules/.bin/webpack src/index.js public/bundle.js`**

Your Terminal should now look like this:

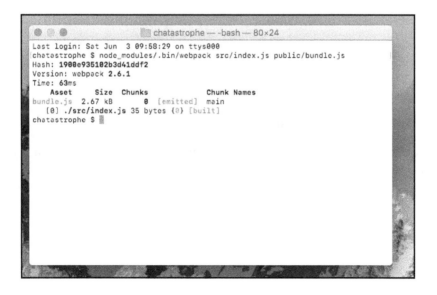

What does this do? Well, it tells Webpack to take the first file and copy it (and everything it needs, that is, every file it requires) into the second file (which Webpack created for us, since it didn't exist).

If you open up the newly created `public/bundle.js`, you'll see a lot of Webpack boilerplate… and at the bottom, our `console.log`.

Okay, so it works; we can require this file in our `index.html` to see our `console.log`, but that's not using Webpack to its full potential. Let's try something else.

# Bundling files

Let's take a look at how Webpack combines our JavaScript files together. Go through the following steps to add a second JavaScript file:

1. In our `src` folder, create another file. Let's call it `index2.js`, for lack of creativity.
2. Inside, add a second `console.log`:

   ```
   console.log('Hello from index2.js!');
   ```

3. Then, back in `index.js` (the first one), we'll require the other file, as follows:

   ```
   require('./index2.js');
   console.log('Hello from index.js!');
   ```

   This basically means that `index.js` now tells Webpack, "Hey, I need this other index!"

4. Okay, let's rerun the same Webpack command as earlier:

   ```
   node_modules/.bin/webpack src/index.js public/bundle.js
   ```

Again, we'll only specify `src/index.js`, but if you look at the console output, you'll see that Webpack now grabs the other file too:

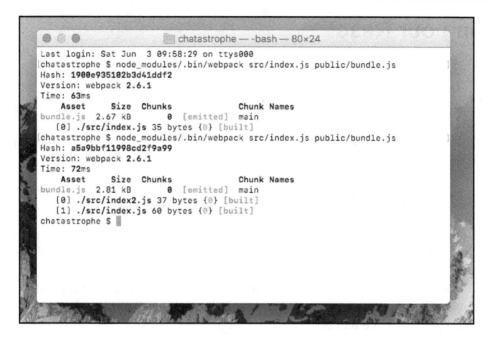

5. Open up `public/bundle.js`, scroll to the bottom, and you'll see both console logs.

   There's the beauty of Webpack. We can now expand our app to contain any number of JavaScript files, and use Webpack to merge them all into one.

6. Okay, let's ensure that those console logs are working. In our `public/index.html`, add another script tag below the other three:

   ```
   <script src="bundle.js"></script>
   ```

7. Reload the page, open up your console, and you'll have this:

# Moving our React

Enough of console logs; now, let's use Webpack to take care of some useful code:

1. Delete our `index2.js`, and delete all code from `index.js`. Then, copy and paste our React code into `index.js`, and delete the first three script tags in the `index.html`.

2. After doing so, you should have only one script tag in your `index.html` (the one for `bundle.js`), and your `index.js` should consist of this line:

   ```
   ReactDOM.render(React.createElement('h1', false, 'Hello from
   React!'), document.getElementById('root'))
   ```

3. Before we run Webpack, though, we have a problem. We deleted the script tags that required React and ReactDOM, but we still need a way to access them in our `index.js`.

4. We can do it in the same way we required `index2.js`, that is, type out `require('../node_modules/react/dist/react.js')`, but that's a lot of typing. Also, we will be using many dependencies from `node_modules` in our code.

5. Fortunately, requiring modules in this way is common, so the `require` function is smart enough to grab a dependency based on the name alone, which means we can add this to the beginning of our `index.js`:

   ```
   var React = require('react');
   var ReactDOM = require('react-dom');
   ```

   We can then use these packages in our code, just as before!

6. Alright, let's try it out. Run Webpack again:

   ```
   node_modules/.bin/webpack src/index.js public/bundle.js
   ```

   It will show the following output:

```
  ●  ●  ●                  chatastrophe — -bash — 80×24
    [1] ./src/index.js 60 bytes {0} [built]
[chatastrophe $ node_modules/.bin/webpack src/index.js public/bundle.js
Hash: 038cd0675ca905a5268f
Version: webpack 2.6.1
Time: 1342ms
      Asset     Size  Chunks                    Chunk Names
bundle.js   738 kB        0  [emitted]  [big]  main
    [5] ./~/react-dom/lib/ReactDOMComponentTree.js 6.27 kB {0} [built]
    [6] ./~/fbjs/lib/ExecutionEnvironment.js 1.06 kB {0} [built]
    [8] ./~/react-dom/lib/ReactInstrumentation.js 601 bytes {0} [built]
   [10] ./~/react-dom/lib/ReactUpdates.js 9.53 kB {0} [built]
   [19] ./~/react/lib/React.js 3.32 kB {0} [built]
   [80] ./~/react-dom/index.js 59 bytes {0} [built]
   [81] ./~/react/react.js 56 bytes {0} [built]
  [111] ./~/react-dom/lib/ReactDOM.js 5.14 kB {0} [built]
  [170] ./~/react/lib/ReactChildren.js 6.19 kB {0} [built]
  [171] ./~/react/lib/ReactClass.js 26.9 kB {0} [built]
  [172] ./~/react/lib/ReactDOMFactories.js 5.53 kB {0} [built]
  [173] ./~/react/lib/ReactPropTypes.js 500 bytes {0} [built]
  [175] ./~/react/lib/ReactPureComponent.js 1.32 kB {0} [built]
  [176] ./~/react/lib/ReactVersion.js 350 bytes {0} [built]
  [181] ./src/index.js 172 bytes {0} [built]
     + 167 hidden modules
chatastrophe $ ▉
```

Now, you can see all the files that Webpack bundles together in our `index.js`: React, all its dependencies, and ReactDOM.

Reload the page and you should see that nothing has changed. However, our application is now much more scalable, and we can organize our files a lot better. When we add a dependency, we no longer need to add another `<script>` tag; we just require it in our code where we're using it.

# Shortcuts

Typing out that long Webpack command is boring and opens us up to errors potentially being made (what if we mistype `bundle.js` and end up generating the wrong file?). Let's simplify that process for our own sanity.

First, let's decide that our `index.js` will be the entry point to our application, which means that it will require all the other files in the application (or rather, it will require a few files that require a few other files, which require a few other files, and so on).

Conversely, our `bundle.js` will be our output file, where all our bundled code goes.

Those two files, therefore, will always be the arguments we give to the Webpack command in our Terminal. Since they won't change, let's configure Webpack to always use them.

In our project folder (not in `src`, but the top-level folder), create a file called `webpack.config.js`. In it, put the following:

```
module.exports = {
  entry:  __dirname + "/src/index.js",
  output: {
   path: __dirname + "/public",
   filename: "bundle.js",
   publicPath: "/",
  }
};
```

We define our entry point as the path to the `index.js` (`__dirname` is a global variable which grabs the current directory, that is, wherever we run the command `webpack`). We then define our output file.

Now, we can simply run `node_modules/.bin/webpack` in our Terminal, with no arguments, and get the same results:

**node_modules/.bin/webpack**

A good improvement, but we're developers, so we're lazy and want to take even more shortcuts. Let's shorten that `node_modules/.bin/webpack` command.

One of the cool features of `npm` is the ability to write scripts to perform commonly used tasks. Let's try it out. In our `package.json`, create a scripts section; within that, make a script named `build`, with a value of the `node_modules/.bin/webpack` command:

```
{
  "name": "chatastrophe",
  "version": "1.0.0",
  "main": "index.js",
  "license": "MIT",
  "scripts": {
    "build": "node_modules/.bin/webpack",
  },
  "dependencies": {
    "react": "15.6.1",
    "react-dom": "15.6.1",
    "webpack": "3.5.4",
  }
}
```

Then, in the Terminal, you can run either `npm run build` or `yarn build`. They do the same thing: run the Webpack command and bundle our files!

Wow, our life is getting easier and easier. Could we be any lazier?

In short, yes.

# Our Dev server

If we want to update our code (say, to change our `h1` to `h2`), we'll have to make the change, rerun `yarn build`, and then reload the page for every single change we want to see. That'll slow us down a lot in our development process.

Ideally, every time we change our JavaScript, the Webpack command will automatically rerun, and will reload the page. What a world of luxury that would be!

Fortunately, there's a package called `webpack-dev-server` for exactly this purpose. To install it, just run `yarn add webpack-dev-server`.

Before we jump in, let's briefly cover how the Dev Server works. It runs a small Node application in the background of our machine, serving up the files in our public folder so that we can see them by visiting `localhost:3000` in our browser. At the same time, it watches the source files of the `bundle.js`, rebundles them when they change, and then reloads the page.

To get it to work, we need to specify which folder we want to serve up (public), and then do some basic configuration.

In our `webpack.config.js`, add the following before the closing squiggly bracket (we have the full code here):

```
devServer: {
  contentBase: "./public",
  historyApiFallback: true,
  inline: true,
}
```

`contentBase` does this, setting `public` as the folder to serve, `historyApiFallback` lets our single-page app seem like a multipage app, and `inline` is the bit that automatically refreshes the page on file changes:

```
module.exports = {
  entry: __dirname + "/src/index.js",
  output: {
   path: __dirname + "/public",
   filename: "bundle.js",
   publicPath: "/"
  },
  devServer: {
    contentBase: "./public",
    historyApiFallback: true,
    inline: true,
  }
};
```

Okay, let's try it. First, we'll add a new script to our `package.json`, called `start`:

```
"scripts": {
  "build": "node_modules/.bin/webpack",
  "start": "node_modules/.bin/webpack-dev-server"
},
```

This will run our Dev Server (ensure that you ran `yarn add webpack-dev-server` first). In your Terminal, type in `yarn start`. You'll see our Webpack compile, and a notice that our app is running on port `8080`. Let's hop over to `http://localhost:8080` in our browser and we should see our application.

The last test is to change the text in our `index.js` from `Hello from React` to `Hello from Webpack!`. Your browser tab should automatically reload and reflect the changes, without you having to rerun the Webpack command.

# Webpack loaders

We're about to step into the future.

So far in this book, we've been using JavaScript in its old form. The language recently (in 2015) got a facelift, with a smattering of conveniences and new functionalities added. This new release is called **ECMAScript 2015**, or **ES6** for short. It's much more enjoyable to use than older JavaScript (ES5), but there's a problem.

All internet browsers are perfectly capable of running JavaScript, but many users are using older browsers that are not yet capable of running ES6. So, as developers, we want to use ES6, but how can we do so and still have our website work on older browsers?

The key is that ES6 doesn't do much that ES5 couldn't do, it just makes it easier to write.

For instance, looping through an array was done like this previously:

```
var arr = [1, 2, 3, 4];
for (var i = 0; i < arr.length; i++) {
  console.log(arr[i]);
}
```

Now, it's done like this:

```
[1, 2, 3, 4].forEach(num => console.log(num));
```

An older browser understands the first one, but not the second, but the code does the same thing. So, all we need to do is convert the second code snippet into the first. This is where Babel comes in. **Babel** is a transpiler tool for JavaScript; think of it as a translator. We give it our beautiful ES6 code, and it converts it into uglier but more browser-friendly ES5 code.

We will stick Babel into our Webpack build process so that when we bundle all our JavaScript files, we also transpile them.

To get started, we will install Babel, along with a bunch of plugins and add-ons for it to make it play nice with React. Stop your Dev server, and then run the following:

```
yarn add babel-core babel-loader babel-preset-es2015 babel-preset-react
babel-plugin-transform-class-properties
```

Yikes, that's a lot of packages all at once! The important one for the next step is `babel-loader`. This is a Webpack loader, and we use it to grab (and then transpile) our JavaScript files before passing them to Webpack for bundling. Let's plug it into Webpack.

In our `webpack.config.js`, make a module object with a loaders array within it:

```
1  module.exports = {
2    entry: __dirname + "/src/index.js",
3    output: {
4      path: __dirname + "/public",
5      filename: "bundle.js"
6    },
7    module: {
8      loaders: [
9
10     ]
11   },
12   devServer: {
13     contentBase: "./public",
14     historyApiFallback: true,
15     inline: true,
16   },
17 };
```

Then, we can define our loader inside the array.

We will make an object with four keys: test, exclude, loader, and query:

- **Test** is what the loader will use to determine which files it should transpile. For Babel, we want to run on all JavaScript files, so our test will be for the files ending with `.js`:

  ```
  test: /\.js$/
  ```

- **Exclude** is what not to run on. We can skip our entire `node_modules` folder, since the packages are already in ES5:

  ```
  exclude: /node_modules/
  ```

- **Loader** is what our loader is called:

  ```
  loader: 'babel-loader'
  ```

- Finally, we'll use **query** to define our presets (what Babel will use to transpile the JavaScript):

  ```
  query: {
    presets: ['es2015','react'],
    plugins: ['transform-class-properties']
  }
  ```

Here's what the full file should look like:

```
module.exports = {
  entry: __dirname + "/src/index.js",
  output: {
   path: __dirname + "/public",
   filename: "bundle.js",
   publicPath: "/"
  },
  module: {
    loaders: [
      {
        test: /\.js$/,
        exclude: /node_modules/,
        loader: 'babel-loader',
        query: {
          presets: ['es2015','react'],
          plugins: ['transform-class-properties']
        }
      },
    ]
  },
  devServer: {
    contentBase: "./public",
    historyApiFallback: true,
    inline: true,
  }
};
```

Run `yarn start` and look for errors. If there aren't any, we can take it for a test drive and write some ES6 code.

# Our first ES6

Let's open up our `src/index.js` and see how we can spice it up.

First, we can replace our `require` calls with the new `import` syntax. It looks like this:

```
import React from 'react';
import ReactDOM from 'react-dom';
```

It's a little cleaner, and it lets us do some cool stuff, which we'll see later.

Do that for both React and ReactDOM, and then we can finally replace our `React.createElement` call.

As you may guess, it would be very unwieldy to build a complex UI by calling `React.createElement` for every HTML element we need. We want the power and functionality of JavaScript, but with the readability of HTML.

Enter JSX; **JSX** is a type of syntax that looks like HTML, but is actually JavaScript underneath. In other words, it compiles down to `React.createElement`, just as our ES6 JavaScript will compile into ES5.

It has some gotchas as well, since it's not true HTML, but we'll get there. The last thing to note is that JSX makes some developers very uncomfortable; they say it looks odd to have HTML inside JavaScript. I don't agree, personally, but it's an opinion thing. Whatever your aesthetic stance, JSX offers a lot of convenience, so let's try it out.

We can simply convert our line of code to this:

```
ReactDOM.render(<h1>Hello from ES6!</h1>, document.getElementById('root'));
```

Run `yarn start` (or, if it's already running, it should automatically refresh). If Babel is working correctly, nothing should change. Our first JSX is done!

We will, of course, work much more with JSX, looking at how it differs from HTML, and what advantages it offers to us as developers. However, for now, let's make our lives even easier.

# Splitting up our app

To organize our app a bit better (and to do some magic in the next section), let's move our JSX into a separate file from our `ReactDOM.render`. This will ensure good separation of concerns throughout our file structure.

Next to `index.js`, in our `src` folder, create a file called `App.js`. Inside, we'll just make a function called `App`, which returns our JSX:

```
import React from 'react';

const App = () => {
  return <h1>Hello from React!!</h1>
};

export default App;
```

Note the `export` statement at the bottom; this means when we import our file, we'll automatically get this function as the default import. We'll see an example of non-default imports down the line, which will make this clearer.

If we jump back to `index.js`, we can now import `App` from `'./App'`. Then, we render it, as shown:

```
import React from 'react';
import ReactDOM from 'react-dom';
import App from './App'

ReactDOM.render(<App />, document.getElementById('root'));
```

Note that we are using it just like an HTML (or rather, JSX) tag. We'll talk more about why in the coming chapters; for now, the important thing is that our app is a bit more organized, with our view logic (the JSX) separate from the render logic (`ReactDOM.render`).

# Hot reloading

We have achieved some pretty big wins for our development process. There's one more convenience I want to add before we move deeper into Webpack configuration.

Imagine an application that consists of a form that pops up in a modal when a user clicks on an **Edit** button. When you reload the page, that modal is closed. Now, imagine that you're the developer trying to fine-tune that form. Your Dev server is reloading the page after every tweak, forcing you to reopen the modal. This is mildly annoying in this case, but think about something like a browser game, where getting back to where you were requires several clicks.

In short, we need a way to reload our JavaScript while still preserving the current state of the application, without reloading the page itself; this is called **hot reloading**. We use Webpack to swap out the bits of our UI that have changed, without reloading everything.

In order to do so, we will use *Dan Abramov's* `react-hot-loader` package. Let's install it and see how we will configure Webpack to play nicely with it.

To install, type `yarn add react-hot-loader@3.0.0`. At the time of writing, version 3 is still in beta; if yarn prompts you to select a beta version of 3.0, pick the latest (for me, I chose beta.7):

```
yarn add react-hot-loader@3.0.0
```

To get it working, we need to do four things:

1. Turn on Webpack's own hot module replacement plugin.
2. Use React Hot Loader as an entry point to our app so that Webpack looks to it for source files.
3. Connect React Hot Loader to Babel.
4. Turn on hot reloading with our Dev Server.

Installing Webpack's HMR plugin is actually quite easy. In our `webpack.config.js`, first require Webpack at the top of the file so that we can access the package:

```
var webpack = require('webpack');
```

 Our Webpack file is not processed by Babel, so we will still use `require` instead of `import`.

Then, above our `devServer` key, add a new key called `plugins`, with an array as the value, which includes `new webpack.HotModuleReplacementPlugin()` as the only item:

```
module: {
  loaders: [
    {
      test: /\.js$/,
      exclude: /node_modules/,
      loader: 'babel-loader',
      query: {
        presets: ['es2015','react'],
        plugins: ['transform-class-properties']
      }
    },
  ]
},
plugins: [
  new webpack.HotModuleReplacementPlugin()
],
devServer: {
  contentBase: "./public",
  historyApiFallback: true,
  inline: true,
}
```

Restart your server to check for errors, and then move on to step 2.

Right now, our `index.js` is our entry point for Webpack; it executes the code in that file and derives from the bundle of the files used in that execution. We want to execute the `react-hot-loader` package first. Let's modify our entry key to be like this:

```
entry: [
  'react-hot-loader/patch',
  __dirname + "/src/index.js"
],
```

To make it work with our Dev server, we need to add a bit more code:

```
entry: [
  'react-hot-loader/patch',
  'webpack-dev-server/client?http://localhost:8080',
  'webpack/hot/only-dev-server',
  __dirname + "/src/index.js"
],
```

This configuration means that Webpack will execute the code in these paths before moving on to our code.

Again, try restarting your server. If there is an error, check for typos; otherwise, onward!

Next, we want to add a Babel plugin so that our hot reloaded files are compiled with `babel-loader`. Just update our Babel configuration, as shown, using the Babel plugin included in `react-hot-loader`:

```
loaders: [
  {
    test: /\.js$/,
    exclude: /node_modules/,
    loader: 'babel-loader',
    query: {
      presets: ['es2015','react'],
      plugins: ['react-hot-loader/babel', 'transform-class-properties']
    }
  },
]
```

We also need to turn on hot reloading with our Dev Server; do so by adding a `hot: true` to our `devServer` config:

```
devServer: {
  contentBase: "./public",
  historyApiFallback: true,
```

```
    inline: true,
    hot: true
},
```

As the last step, we need to add a bit of code to our `index.js`. Add the following to the bottom of the file:

```
if (module.hot) {
  module.hot.accept('./App', () => {
    const NextApp = require('./App').default;
    ReactDOM.render(
     <App/>,
     document.getElementById('root')
    );
  });
}
```

The preceding code basically sends a new version of our app to `ReactDOM.render` when the files change.

Okay, let's give it a shot. Restart your server, and then open up `localhost:8080`. Try editing the text `Hello from React!`, and watch as the HTML updates without the page ever reloading; neat.

**Hot Module Replacement** will make our lives much easier, especially once we start building our app with different states--states that reloading the page will reset.

# Building for production

So far, we've been entirely focused on using Webpack in a development context, but we also need to think about deploying our app to production, and what that may involve.

When we send our app out to the World Wide Web, we don't want to send anything unnecessary (remember that our goal is performance); we want to deploy the bare minimum.

Here's what we need:

- An `index.html` page (minified)
- A CSS file (minified)
- A JavaScript file (minified)
- All image assets
- An asset manifest (a list of the preceding static files)

We have some of these, but not all. Let's work on using Webpack to automatically generate a `build` folder with all of these, which we can deploy later.

First, a minified `index.html`. We want Webpack to take our `public/index.html` file, minify it, add the appropriate script and CSS links automatically, and then add that to a `build` folder.

Since our Webpack process for production will be different from development, let's make a duplicate of our `webpack.config.js` and name it `webpack.config.prod.js`. For most of the rest of the chapter, we'll work with `webpack.config.prod.js`, not `webpack.config.js`.

First things first, delete the `devServer` key from `webpack.config.prod.js`. We won't use a Dev server in production, nor will we use hot reloading. We need to delete the two `devServer` specific lines under `entry`, and the hot reloading line, so that it now looks like this:

```
entry: __dirname + "/src/index.js",
```

Also, inside our `webpack.config.prod.js`, let's specify that our output folder is now `chatastrophe/build` by changing this line under output:

```
path: __dirname + "/public",
```

It needs to be changed to this:

```
path: __dirname + "/build",
```

We'll also want to add a `publicPath`, so our `index.html` in `build` will know to look for the bundled JavaScript in the same folder:

```
output: {
  path: __dirname + "/build",
  filename: "bundle.js",
  publicPath: './'
},
```

Let's set our environment to production so that React doesn't display its (helpful, in development) warnings. We can also remove `HotModuleReplacementPlugin`:

```
plugins: [
  new webpack.DefinePlugin({
    'process.env': {
```

```
        NODE_ENV: JSON.stringify('production')
      }
    }),
  ],
```

Next, we will use a new Webpack plugin, called `HtmlWebpackPlugin`. It does what it sounds like--packs down HTML for us! Let's install it with `yarn add html-webpack-plugin`, and then add it with the following options:

```
plugins: [
  new webpack.DefinePlugin({
    'process.env': {
      NODE_ENV: JSON.stringify('production')
    }
  }),
  new HtmlWebpackPlugin({
    inject: true,
    template: __dirname + "/public/index.html",
    minify: {
      removeComments: true,
      collapseWhitespace: true,
      removeRedundantAttributes: true,
      useShortDoctype: true,
      removeEmptyAttributes: true,
      removeStyleLinkTypeAttributes: true,
      keepClosingSlash: true,
      minifyJS: true,
      minifyCSS: true,
      minifyURLs: true,
    },
  }),
],
```

Don't forget to require it at the top of `webpack.config.prod.js`, just like we required Webpack:

```
var HtmlWebpackPlugin = require('html-webpack-plugin');
```

Time to give it a test! In your `package.json`, update our build script to use our new config, as follows:

```
"build": "node_modules/.bin/webpack --config webpack.config.prod.js",
```

Then, run `yarn build`.

You should see a `build` folder appear in your project directory. If you open `build/index.html`, you'll see that it's nice and mushed together. However, there's a problem; in that squashed code, you should see two script tags, both requiring `bundle.js`.

That is the result of the `inject` option we specified earlier with `HtmlWebpackPlugin`. The plugin adds the script tag for us! How convenient, except that we already added it in `public/index.html` ourselves.

Here's a simple solution--let's copy our `HtmlWebpackPlugin` configuration (and require statement) over to `webpack.config.js` (our original configuration file). However, we can remove the `minify` key and all its options, since that's not necessary in development:

```
// webpack.config.js
plugins: [
  new webpack.HotModuleReplacementPlugin(),
  new HtmlWebpackPlugin({
    inject: true,
    template: __dirname + '/public/index.html',
  })
],
```

Then, delete the script tag from `public/index.html` and try `yarn start` again to test whether our development environment is working, and `yarn build` to test our production build.

Okay, we have a minified HTML file in our build, and we have improved our development start process a bit as well. The next task is to ensure that our CSS is minified and copied into our build folder as well.

In our webpack configuration (both production and development), we used `babel-loader` to load our JavaScript files in; we will do something similar with CSS.

To do so, we will combine two loaders: `css-loader` and `style-loader`.

 You can read more about why it's recommended to use both on the style-loader GitHub page at `https://github.com/webpack-contrib/style-loader`.

Install both with the following:

```
yarn add css-loader style-loader
```

Let's add them to both our `webpack.config.prod.js` and `webpack.config.js`, by adding the following code under our `babel-loader` configuration:

```
module: {
  loaders: [
    {
      test: /\.js$/,
      exclude: /node_modules/,
      loader: 'babel-loader',
      query: {
        presets: ['es2015','react'],
        plugins: ['react-hot-loader/babel']
      }
    },
    {
      test: /\.css$/,
      use: [
        { loader: "style-loader" },
        { loader: "css-loader" }
      ]
    }
  ]
},
```

What these plugins do is take a CSS file required by our React code and turn it into a `<style>` tag injected into our HTML. Right now, that won't do much for us, since our CSS is sitting in our `public/assets` folder. Let's move it to `src`, then require it in `App.js`:

```
import React from 'react';
import './app.css';

const App = () => {
  return <h1>Hello from React!!</h1>
};

export default App;
```

Then, we can delete our link tag from our `public/index.html` and restart our server.

If we inspect the head of our HTML in our browser, we should see a `<style>` tag with all our CSS inside. Neat!:

```
<!DOCTYPE html>
<html lang="en">
▶ #shadow-root (open)
▼ <head>
    <meta charset="utf-8">
    <meta name="viewport" content="width=device-width, initial-scale=1">
    <link rel="shortcut icon" href="assets/favicon.ico" type="image/x-icon">
  ▶ <style type="text/css">…</style>  == $0
  </head>
▶ <body>…</body>
</html>
```

Now, you may notice when we refresh the page, that there's a flash of unstyled content; this is a consequence of our app now requiring React to boot up before adding styling. We'll address that issue in the coming chapters, rest assured.

Run `yarn build` and take a look at `bundle.js`. If you search for "Start initial styles" you'll see where our CSS is bundled in our JavaScript. Also, note how relatively readable our JavaScript is compared to our HTML. The next step is to take care of minifying it!

Fortunately, doing so is quite easy. We just add another Webpack plugin to our `production` file. After `HtmlWebpackPlugin`, add the following:

```
plugins: [
  new HtmlWebpackPlugin({
    inject: true,
    template: __dirname + '/public/index.html',
    minify: {
      removeComments: true,
      collapseWhitespace: true,
      removeRedundantAttributes: true,
      useShortDoctype: true,
      removeEmptyAttributes: true,
      removeStyleLinkTypeAttributes: true,
      keepClosingSlash: true,
      minifyJS: true,
      minifyCSS: true,
      minifyURLs: true
    }
  }),
  new webpack.optimize.UglifyJsPlugin({
    compress: {
      warnings: false,
      reduce_vars: false
    },
    output: {
      comments: false
    },
    sourceMap: true
  })
]
```

Run `yarn build` again, and you should see that our `bundle.js` has become a single line. This is not great for humans, but much faster for the browser.

Okay, we're getting closer to the end. Next, we want to ensure that all our asset files get copied over to our `build` folder.

We can do so by adding another loader to our Webpack config, called `file-loader`. We'll install it with `yarn add file-loader@0.11.2`. Let's see what the code looks like (note that this is only for our `webpack.config.prod.js` file):

```
module: {
  loaders: [
    {
      test: /\.js$/,
      exclude: /node_modules/,
      loader: 'babel-loader',
      query: {
        presets: ['es2015', 'react'],
        plugins: ['react-hot-loader/babel', 'transform-class-properties']
      }
    },
    {
      test: /\.css$/,
      use: [{ loader: 'style-loader' }, { loader: 'css-loader' }]
    },
    {
      exclude: [/\.html$/, /\.(js|jsx)$/, /\.css$/, /\.json$/],
      loader: 'file-loader',
      options: {
        name: 'static/media/[name].[ext]'
      }
    }</strong>
  ]
},
```

Note that we're excluding HTML, CSS, JSON, and JS files. These are covered by our other loaders, so we don't want to duplicate files.

We're also putting these assets in a `static` folder, just like our `assets` folder in our `public` folder.

However, `file-loader` will only apply to those files required by our JavaScript code. We have our favicon and icon, which are currently only used in our `index.html`, so Webpack won't find them.

To do so, we will use JavaScript instead of Webpack (since Webpack focuses only on our `src` folder).

# Creating a custom script

Make a new folder in the root of your directory and name it `scripts`. Inside, make a file called `copy_assets.js`.

In here, we will copy everything in `public` to `build`, excluding our `index.html`.

To do this (you guessed it), we need one more package; run `yarn add fs-extra`.

Then, require it inside `copy_assets.js`, as illustrated:

```
var fs = require('fs-extra');
```

`fs-extra` is a package used for manipulating files in a Node environment. It has a method called `copySync`, which we'll use here.

The code is rather straightforward:

```
fs.copySync('public', 'build', {
  dereference: true,
  filter: file => file !== 'public/index.html'
});
```

This says copy everything in the `public` folder to the `build` folder, except the `index.html` file.

> If you have a `bundle.js` in your `public` folder from our previous Webpack config, you can delete it now.

Now, to run this command whenever we build, add it to the build script in `package.json`:

```
"scripts": {
  "build": "node scripts/copy_assets.js && node_modules/.bin/webpack --
config
    webpack.config.prod.js",
  "start": "node_modules/.bin/webpack-dev-server"
},
```

It's a good idea to put the `copy_assets` command before our Webpack command, just to ensure that we don't accidentally copy any JavaScript assets in `public` without transpiling them.

## Making an asset manifest

As the last step, we want a list of all the static assets that we're generating. This will be useful down the line, once we start caching them to save load times. Fortunately, it's an easy step, another plugin!

`yarn add webpack-manifest-plugin` and add it to `webpack.config.prod.js`, under plugins, with the following configuration:

```
var ManifestPlugin = require('webpack-manifest-plugin');
// Then, under plugins:
new ManifestPlugin({
  fileName: 'asset-manifest.json',
}),
```

Okay, let's try it all together. Run `yarn build` and then open `index.html` in the browser. It should look exactly the same as running `yarn start`. You should also see an `index.html`, a `bundle.js`, an `asset-manifest.json`, and an `assets` folder in our `build` folder.

# Summary

Whew! That was a lot of configuration. The good news is that now we are completely ready to start writing React, and build our application. That's what we'll move on to next!

In this chapter, we covered everything to do with Webpack, adding in a bunch of convenient features to speed up our development. In the next chapter, we'll start the development process, and begin constructing our React application. This is where the fun begins!

# 3
# Our App's Login Page

We've spent the last couple of chapters getting our application completely set up for development with React. Now, let's go full steam ahead with building our application.

In this chapter, we will create our application's login page in React. By the end, you should feel comfortable with basic React syntax.

We will cover the following key React concepts:

- Separating the UI into components
- Writing JSX
- Functional components versus class components
- Component state
- Creating reusable components

## What is a React component?

A **React component**, at the most basic level, is a piece of the user interface, more specifically, a section of UI devoted to a single purpose.

With React, your UI is split up into sections, sections within those sections, then sections within those, and so on; you get the picture. Each section is its own component, and lives in a separate file.

The beauty of this system may not be obvious now, but once we dive into it, you'll see how it makes our application much more comprehendible, that is, easy for us to understand and navigate as we're developing. We'll only be building a small application with a few components. The effect increases as your application grows to hundreds of components.

Let's look at a quick example of splitting a UI into components. Here's the online store of Packt, the publishers of this book:

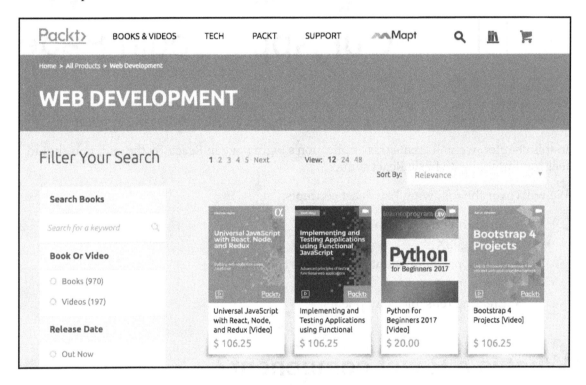

If we were to rebuild this in React, we would start by dividing the UI into meaningful sections. Which parts are concerned with different purposes?

Note that there is no single correct answer to this question; different developers will do it differently, but here's a division that makes sense to me: splitting it up into a **FilterControl**, a **SearchBar**, and a **ResultsGrid**:

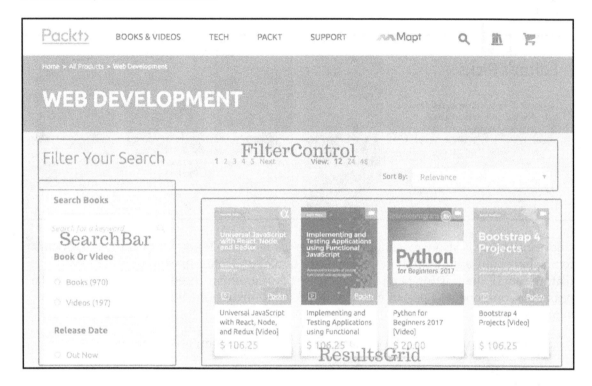

Here's my thinking--the **FilterControl** (at the top) has to do with sorting and pagination, the **SearchSideBar** is all about searching for specific results, and the **ResultsGrid** is all about displaying matching results. Each has a very specific and distinct purpose.

Then, within those three components, we can make smaller divisions. Each book in the **ResultsGrid** can be a **BookCard** component, with a **BookInfo** and **BookImage** component within it, and so on.

How fine-grained we want to make these divisions is up to us. Generally, a greater number of smaller components is better, but one does have to write more boilerplate the more components one decides to write.

The other advantage of React componentization is reusability. Let's say that, within our **ResultsGrid**, we make a **BookCard** component for each result. Then, on the Packt home page, we can reuse the same component! No more rewriting the same code twice in two places:

Code reusability is also why smaller components are better. If you build your components to maximize reusability (to fit in the greatest number of contexts), you can build new features out of the existing parts. This increases development speed and ease. We'll build a reuseable component as part of our login form, and plug it elsewhere as our application expands.

Let's jump into our App.js file and take a look at the first component that we built:

```
import React, { Component } from 'react';
import './app.css';

const App = () => {
  return <h1>Hello from React!!</h1>
};

export default App;
```

Our App component is a function that returns a bit of JSX. That's it. This is a very handy way of thinking of React components, as functions that return part of the view. By calling certain functions in a certain order, we construct our UI.

It does, of course, get a bit more complicated than that. However, if you ever feel overwhelmed by the React syntax and concepts, come back to this core principle: React components are just functions that return parts of the UI.

# Controversies and Separation of Concerns

When React first emerged on the scene, it was very controversial (and for many people, it still is). The core point of concern for many developers was JSX, having what appeared to be HTML in the middle of JavaScript code.

For years, developers had been writing their HTML, CSS, and JavaScript in separate files. React violated that tradition. Some developers accused the library of violating the programming principle of **Separation of Concerns** (**SoC**)--the idea that code should be separated into files, each intended to do one thing. In this sense, they argued that you should have an HTML file, a CSS file, and a JavaScript file—no mingling of HTML and JavaScript.

What the React developers pointed out is that separating files based on type (HTML versus JavaScript) was a separation of technology, not a Separation of Concerns. The HTML and JavaScript were both concerned with rendering a functional UI—they belonged together.

React proposed that if you had a button, both the HTML structure of the button and what made it functional (what happened when it was clicked on) should live in the same file, since that was all the same concern.

Thus, the important thing to remember with React is the idea of Separation of Concerns—you can draw lines between your components based on what their purpose is.

The missing piece of all of this is, of course, CSS. Shouldn't it be in the same file as well? Many think so, but a mature solution to do so has yet to emerge. You can read more about CSS in JS at `https://medium.freecodecamp.org/css-in-javascript-the-future-of-component-based-styling-70b161a79a32`.

# Class components versus functional components

We just defined React components as functions that return a piece of the UI. This is a useful way of thinking about them, and is certainly true for our `App` component. However, there's another way of writing React components.

Right now, our `App` component is a functional component. This means it's literally written as a function, but you can also write components as JavaScript classes. These are called **class-based** or **stateful** components (we'll talk about the stateful part in a bit).

JavaScript classes are a new feature of ES6. They work in a similar (but not identical) way to classes in other languages. We won't delve too deep into them here, but for our purpose, you can do the following:

- Have a class extend another class (and inherit its properties)
- Create an instance of a class with the new keyword (that is, instantiate it)

Let's see an example by converting our App component into a class-based component.

Every class component must do two things: it must extend the Component class from the React library, and it must have a render method.

Let's start by importing the Component class from React:

```
import React, { Component } from 'react';
```

For those of you unfamiliar with this syntax, it's an example of object destructuring in ES6. Consider the following:

```
const property = object.property;
```

Object destructuring turns the preceding code into this, which saves some typing, but does the same thing:

```
const { property } = object;
```

Anyway, now that we've imported our Component class, let's make a class that extends it; delete our App function, and write the following:

```
class App extends Component {

}
```

JavaScript classes function a lot like objects. They can have properties that are either values or functions (called methods). As we said earlier, we need a render method. Here's what that looks like:

```
class App extends Component {
  render() {

  }
}
```

What does the `render` method do? In essence, when we wrote our `App` as a functional component, it consisted solely of a `render` method. The whole thing was just a big `render()`. So, the render method does what we expect from a React component: it returns a bit of the view:

```
class App extends Component {
  render() {
    return <h1>Hello from React!!</h1>;
  }
}
```

If you start up the app (or if it's already running), you'll note that nothing has changed at all.

So, what is the difference between a class component and a functional component?

A best practice is to try to make as many small, functional components as possible in your application. They're a bit faster performance-wise, and the React team has expressed an interest in optimizing the library for functional components. They're also easier to understand.

However, class components give us a lot of handy functionality. They can have properties, which we then use in the `render` method:

```
class App extends Component {
  greeting = 'Hello from React!!';

  render() {
    return <h1>{this.greeting}</h1>;
  }
}
```

We can call methods from the `render` method:

```
class App extends Component {
  logGreeting = () => {
    console.log('Hello!');
  }

  render() {
    this.logGreeting()
    return <h1>Hello from React!!</h1>;
  }
}
```

As we discussed earlier, classes can be instantiated (in syntax such as `const app = new App()`). This is what React does in our `ReactDOM.render` call; it instantiates our `App` and then calls the `render` method to get the JSX.

Therefore, it's still useful to think of React components as functions that return bits of view. Class components just add a little extra functionality wrapped around that `render` function.

# Our second component

We've made one React component; let's make another!

As we discussed earlier, the goal of this chapter is to create our application's login page. First, let's create a folder called `components/` in our `src` folder, and then inside, let's create a file called `LoginContainer.js`.

 If you still have the folder from our Chapter 2, *Getting Started with Webpack*, with `Component1.js`, `Component2.js`, and `Component3.js`, feel free to delete those files now.

Our `LoginContainer` will be another class component, for reasons that we'll look at down the road. Just as with our app, let's set up a basic class component skeleton:

```
import React, { Component } from 'react';

class LoginContainer extends Component {
  render() {

  }
}

export default LoginContainer;
```

Let's test out rendering our component before we dive any further in. Return a simple `<h1>Hello from LoginContainer</h1>` from our `render` method; then, let's jump back to our `App.js`.

I'm a bit of a stickler for code organization, so before we go on, let's move our `App.js` inside our `components` folder. This also means that we'll have to change our import statement in `index.js` to the following:

```
import App from './components/App';
```

Also, move our `app.css` inside the `components` folder, and then change our hot reloader configuration inside `index.js`:

```
if (module.hot) {
  module.hot.accept('./components/App', () => {
    const NextApp = require('./components/App').default;
    ReactDOM.render(
      <App/>,
      document.getElementById('root')
    );
  });
}
```

Now that all our components are living together in the same folder, it's much better.

Inside `App.js`, we first import the `LoginContainer`:

```
import LoginContainer from './LoginContainer';
```

Then, we `render` it instead of the `<h1>`:

```
import React, { Component } from 'react';
import LoginContainer from './LoginContainer';
import './app.css';


class App extends Component {
  render() {
    return <LoginContainer />
  }
}

export default App;
```

Flip back to the app, and you should see the **Hello from LoginContainer** of our new component:

As we shall see as we build more components, our `App` will be a wrapper for our main `Container` component. It'll be, in essence, a container for our Containers. Inside `App.js`, let's wrap our `LoginContainer` in a `div#container` for CSS purposes:

```
class App extends Component {
  render() {
    return (
      <div id="container" className="inner-container">
        <LoginContainer />
      </div>
    );
  }
}
```

Alright, getting back to `LoginContainer.js`, let's write some JSX!

Delete our `<h1>` tag and replace it with the following:

```
class LoginContainer extends Component {
  render() {
    return (
      <div id="LoginContainer" className="inner-container">

      </div>
    );
  }
}
```

This is a pattern I really like--having most React components wrapped in a `div` with an `id` of the class name; it's just a preference, though (a preference you'll have to follow for this book, since I wrote the CSS!).

 Note the brackets around the JSX! This format makes multiline JSX much more readable.

The essence of our login form is, of course, a form. This form will handle both login and signup. Here's the basic JSX:

```
class LoginContainer extends Component {
    render() {
      return (
        <div id="LoginContainer" className="inner-container">
          <form>
            <p>Sign in or sign up by entering your email and password.</p>
            <input
              type="text"
              placeholder="Your email" />
            <input
              type="password"
              placeholder="Your password" />
            <button className="red light" type="submit">Login</button>
          </form>
        </div>
      )
   }
}
```

In the preceding JSX, you may note that I wrote `className` instead of class for the `<button>`. Remember that I said JSX had a few caveats? This is one: since class is a protected keyword in JavaScript, we can't use it, so we use `className` instead. You'll get used to it in no time.

On that note, pay attention to the `ID` and `className` in the preceding JSX, otherwise your CSS won't look spiffy.

Above our form, we'll write a basic header with our logo:

```
<div id="LoginContainer" className="inner-container">
  <div id="Header">
    <img src="/assets/icon.png" alt="logo" />
    <h1>Chatastrophe</h1>
  </div>
  <form>
```

Your app should now look like this (if you haven't done so, delete the `<h1>` and `<img>` tags from `index.html`):

Looks pretty, but what does it do?

# State in React

Every React component has something called **state.** You can think of this as the configuration of the component at a certain point of time.

Take, for example, a heart icon that turns red when you click on it, as in the case of Twitter. The button has two states: **unclicked** and **clicked**. Clicking on the button causes its state, and thus its appearance, to change.

That's the flow in React; user actions or events cause the component state to change, which causes the component's appearance to change.

The preceding statement comes with an enormous helping of "Well, not always…," but it's a useful starting point to understand state:

```
User event -> State change -> Appearance change
```

Let's add some `state` to our `LoginContainer`, and then go from there.

State is easy to define; it's an object that is the property of the class. We can define it as shown:

```
class LoginContainer extends Component {
  state = { text: 'Hello from state!' }

  render() {
```

We always define `state` at the top of our component.

We can then access our `state` right in the `render` method:

```
class LoginContainer extends Component {
  state = { text: 'Hello from state!' };

  render() {
    return (
      <div id="LoginContainer" className="inner-container">
        <div id="Header">
          <img src="/assets/icon.png" alt="logo" />
          <h1>{this.state.text}</h1>
        </div>
```

In the preceding code, the curly braces inside JSX mean we're inserting some Javascript code.

This is how we initialize our `state`, but this state isn't very useful, since there's no mechanism for changing it.

What we need to do is to provide a way to respond to user events, and modify the state based on them.

What if the text changed when the user clicked on **Hello from state!**?

Let's add an `onClick` property to our h1 tag, as follows:

```
<h1 onClick={this.handleClick}>{this.state.text}</h1>
```

It references a method on our class called `handleClick`, which we can define as shown:

```
class LoginContainer extends Component {
  state = { text: 'Hello from state!' };

  handleClick = () => {
    this.setState({ text: 'State changed!' });
  };

  render() {
```

Inside `handleClick`, we want to change our state. We can do that in React via a function called `this.setState`, into which we pass the new state object.

Try it out! When you click on **Hello from state!**, it should immediately change to the new text.

So, how does this work? What `setState` does is to take the object passed in as an argument and merge it into the current state (if you have multiple properties in state but only pass in an object with one property to `setState`, it'll change only that property, rather than overwriting the rest). Then, it calls the `render()` method again, and our component is updated in the DOM to reflect the new state.

If this seems confusing, don't worry, we have a couple more examples to go through, so you'll get a bit more practice with component state.

Our `LoginContainer` will have two pieces of state, one to go with each `<input>` tag. We will store what the user types in the email and password fields in state so that when they submit the form, we can access them.

"Hold on Scott," you may say, "Why don't we just reach into the DOM and grab the value of each input when the user submits the form, the jQuery way?"

We can certainly do that, but it will break the React flow, which is as follows:

```
User edits input -> Update state -> Re-render input to reflect new value.
```

This way, our input's value is stored in state and the view is kept in sync with it, rather than having our input's value stored as a property of a DOM element, and accessed when needed.

The advantage of this approach may not seem obvious at this point, but it makes our code much more explicit and understandable.

So, in the preceding flow, we need to update our state whenever the user changes an input. First, let's change how our state initializes:

```
state = { email: '', password: '' };
```

Then, let's delete `handleClick` and add the `handleEmailChange` and `handlePasswordChange` methods to our component:

```
handleEmailChange = (event) => {
  this.setState({ email: event.target.value });
};
```

```
handlePasswordChange = (event) => {
  this.setState({ password: event.target.value });
};
```

The preceding methods take in an event (the user typing in the field), grab the value from the event, and then set state to that value.

Again, note that we don't have to define both the email and password every time we call setState; it will merge in the changes to the existing state object without overwriting the other values.

Okay, now the last step. Let's add the onChange properties to our inputs, which call our change handlers. Another crucial step is that our input's value must be derived from state. We can do so like this:

```
<input
  type="text"
  onChange={this.handleEmailChange}
  value={this.state.email}
  placeholder="Your email"
/>
<input
  type="password"
  onChange={this.handlePasswordChange}
  value={this.state.password}
  placeholder="Your password"
/>
```

 You can reset your h1 to <h1>Chatastrophe</h1>.

If everything worked out, you should note no change in how your input functions (if there's a typo in your code, you won't be able to type in one or the other). Let's ensure that it's actually working by adding a handler for when our form submits:

```
<form onSubmit={this.handleSubmit}>
```

And our method:

```
handleSubmit = (event) => {
  event.preventDefault();
  console.log(this.state);
};
```

The preceding method will just log out the state for us when the user submits the form (clicks on the button), and prevent the form from actually submitting.

Try typing in both fields and then click on **Submit**. You should see a console log with the state object:

```
Object { email: "email@email.com", password: "asdfas" }
```

We did it! Our first React component with state.

I hope you've gotten a sense of the React data flow. Our application has state (stored in different components), which updates in response to events (often user-initiated), which causes parts of our application to rerender in response to the new state:

```
Events -> State changes -> Re-render.
```

It's a simple pattern once you wrap your head around it, and makes it easy to trace why your application looks the way it does at any point of time.

# Reusing components

There's one more change I want to make before we finish up with our LoginContainer skeleton.

We talked earlier about making React components reusable, so you can implement the same code in multiple places in your application. We should try to split our UI into as many small and reusable pieces as possible to save us time, and I see a great candidate in our LoginContainer.

LoginContainer won't be our only container. In the next few chapters, we'll create new pages with different content, but we want them to have the same look, and we'll want to have the Chatastrophe logo and title at the top in the same place as it is now.

What I propose is that we make a new Header component that we can save for future use.

Now, we made our LoginContainer a class component because we needed to use state and methods. Our header, on the other hand, won't have any state or functionality; it's literally just a piece of UI. The best choice is to make it a functional component, because we can.

The rule for a class versus a functional component is essentially make a component functional wherever you can, unless you need state or methods.

Inside our `src/` components folder, make a new file called `Header.js`. Then, we can create the skeleton of a functional component. Copy and paste the relevant `div#Header` from `LoginContainer` and add it as the `return` statement:

```
import React from 'react';

const Header = () => {
  return (
    <div id="Header">
      <img src="/assets/icon.png" alt="logo" />
      <h1>Chatastrophe</h1>
    </div>
  );
};

export default Header;
```

Now, back in our `LoginContainer`, we want to import our header, as illustrated:

```
import Header from './Header';
```

Then we can replace the `div#Header` with a simple `<Header />` tag:

```
render() {
  return (
    <div id="LoginContainer" className="inner-container">
      <Header />
      <form onSubmit={this.handleSubmit}>
```

Another JSX gotcha--all JSX tags must be closed. You can't just use `<Header>`.

That's it! That's all it takes to make a small, reusable component. Our `LoginContainer` now looks cleaner, and we've saved ourselves some typing down the road.

Our login form looks fantastic, but there's a problem. As you demo it for the team at Chatastrophe headquarters (the team having somehow swelled to twenty, despite you being the only developer), an intern raises her hand--"How does it actually, you know, work?"

# Summary

We created our first stateful React component, a login form. We learned all about React components, and best practices for creating them. We then built our login form and covered how to handle changes to the form, updating our state.

Unfortunately, a login form that only logs out the email and password isn't that useful (or secure!). Our next step will be to set up the backend of our application so that users can actually create accounts and log in.

# 4
# Easy Backend Setup With Firebase

Our application looks pretty, but it doesn't do that much. We have a login form that doesn't let users actually log in.

In this chapter, we'll get started on the backend of our application. In our case, that means setting up a database to save users and their messages. In one chapter, we will cover everything we need to let our users create accounts and log in. We'll also dive deeper into React and component state. We'll learn the following things:

- What Firebase is
- Gotchas and problems to look out for
- How to deploy our application
- User authentication (signup and login)
- React life cycle methods

Let's get to it!

## What is Firebase?

Building a progressive web app is, for the most part, a frontend process. PWAs care little for how they consume data from a backend API (unless it impedes performance, of course). We want to keep the backend setup for our application minimal; for that, we turn to Firebase.

**Firebase** is a project by Google designed to help developers build apps without worrying about backend infrastructure. It operates on the freemium model, based on the amount of requests your backend has to respond to as well as the amount of storage you need. For our purposes, it is the perfect fit for quickly developing a small prototype. When our app scales, the Chatastrophe executive board assures us, "money won't be an issue."

What does Firebase provide? Of interest to us is a database, a hosting solution, and built-in authentication. Beyond that, it also offers something called **Cloud Functions**, which are snippets of code automatically run in response to certain events. We'll be working with Cloud Functions once we add push notifications to our application. For now, we want to add some authentication to our login form so that users can sign up and log in to Chatastrophe.

If you have a Google account (via Google Plus or Gmail, for example) you can log in to Firebase with those credentials, or create a new account; that's all we need to get started.

# Firebase gotchas

Firebase is a useful tool, but it does have some caveats.

One of the big selling points (for us especially) is its real-time database. This means that changes to the data by one user are automatically pushed to all users. We don't have to check whether a new chat message has been created; each instance of the application will be instantly informed.

The database also has offline persistence, which means our users can read their messages even when they're offline (which, if you remember, fulfills one of the user stories we outlined earlier). Firebase uses local caching to achieve this.

So, what's the downside? The Firebase database is a NoSQL database, and has a specific syntax that may seem strange to developers more used to SQL databases. The process is similar to a SQL database (with the major **CRUD** actions--**Create**, **Read**, **Update**, and **Delete**-- applying to data), but it may not be as intuitive.

The other gotcha with Firebase is that it is not (at the time of writing) optimized for **Single-Page Applications** (**SPAs**) like those built with React. We'll have to do a couple of workarounds to get everything running smoothly with our React application.

All that said, however, Firebase will save us a lot of time in comparison to setting up our own backend server/hosting solution, and it's a pleasure to use for personal projects; this is definitely something worth learning.

# Setting up

Here's how we'll get going with Firebase:

1. We'll go to the Firebase console.
2. From there, we'll create a project.
3. We'll name our lovely little project.
4. We'll get the code necessary to integrate it into our app.
5. We'll add that code to `index.html`.
6. We'll make Firebase available as a global variable.

If you're ready to get started, let's do it:

1. Once you've created or logged in to your Google account, head over to `https://firebase.google.com/`. In the top-right corner of your screen, you should see a button titled **GO TO CONSOLE**:

2. From the Firebase console, we want to **Add Project**. Click on the icon:

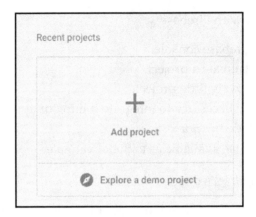

3. For **Project Name**, choose `chatastrophe` (all lowercase), and then select your **Country/Region**.

4. Firebase should take you directly to the project page once that's done. From there, click on the link that says **Add Firebase to your web app**:

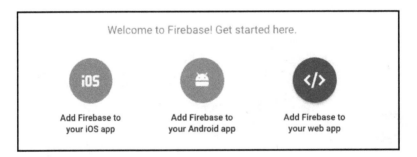

5. Copy and paste the code it gives you into your `public/index.html`, before the closing `</body>` tag:

```
<body>
  <div id="root"></div>
  <script
src="https://www.gstatic.com/firebasejs/4.1.2/firebase.js"></script
>
  <script>
    // Initialize Firebase
    var config = {
      apiKey: /* API KEY HERE */,
      authDomain: "chatastrophe-77bac.firebaseapp.com",
```

```
        databaseURL: "https://chatastrophe-77bac.firebaseio.com",
        projectId: "chatastrophe-77bac",
        storageBucket: "chatastrophe-77bac.appspot.com",
        messagingSenderId: "85734589405"
      };
      firebase.initializeApp(config);
    </script>
  </body>
```

6. Lastly, we need to make our Firebase application available to the rest of our app. At the bottom of the script tag, just before the `firebase.initializeApp(config)` line, add the following:

```
window.firebase = firebase;
```

This code stores our Firebase setup on the `window` object, so we can access it in the rest of our JavaScript.

If you're not using source control (GitHub or Bitbucket, for example) or are using a private repository to store your code, you can skip to the next section. For the rest of us, we need to do some work to ensure that we don't display our `config.apiKey` to the entire world (a recipe for malicious use).

# Hiding our API key

We need to move our API key and `messagingSenderId` to a separate file, and then ensure that the file is not checked into Git:

1. To do so, create a file in `public/` called `secrets.js`. In that file, place the following:

```
window.apiKey = "YOUR-API-KEY"
messagingSenderId = "YOUR-SENDER-ID"
```

Again, we're taking advantage of the globally accessible window object to store the key. For those of you new to JavaScript, note that it is not good practice to abuse the window object; only use it when absolutely necessary.

2. To use this key in `index.html`, we can add the following above all the other script tags:

```
<script src="/secrets.js"></script>
```

3. Then, in our Firebase initialization:

```
<script>
  // Initialize Firebase
  var config = {
    apiKey: window.apiKey,
    // ...rest of config
    messagingSenderId: window.messagingSenderId
  };
```

4. As the last step, we need to tell Git to ignore the `secrets.js` file. You can do so by modifying our `.gitignore` file in the project base, adding the following line:

```
/public/secrets.js
```

All done! We can now commit and push up freely.

# Deploying Firebase

As I mentioned earlier, Firebase comes with a baked-in deployment solution. Let's get our app up and working on the real live web! Here's how to do it:

1. To do so, we'll first need to install the Firebase command-line tools:

   **`npm install -g firebase-tools`**

   Don't forget the `-g`. This flag installs the tools globally on your machine.

2. The next step is to log in to our Firebase tools:

   **`firebase login`**

3. To complete our Firebase tools setup, we can now initialize our app as a Firebase project, similar to what we did with npm. Ensure that you run this from the root of the project folder:

   **`firebase init`**

In the first question it then prompts you for, use the arrow keys and the *Spacebar* to select both **Functions** and **Hosting**. We will use Firebase's Cloud Functions later on. Don't select **Database**, that's for configuring database rules locally; we'll rely on the Firebase console instead.

Your selections should look like this:

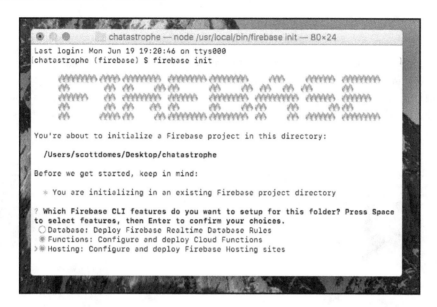

When it asks for a default Firebase project, select `chatastrophe`(or whatever you named this project in the Firebase console).

For the question **Do you want to install dependencies with npm now?**, enter **y**.

Next, it'll ask you what folder you want to use as your public directory. Enter `build`, not `public`. Firebase is asking what folder to use to deploy your project; we want our final compiled build, including our transpiled JavaScript and therefore, we want the `build` folder.

Let's move to the next question now! Do we want to configure our app as a single-page application? Heck yes. Decline overwriting `index.html` though (however, no worries if you say yes; we regenerate our `build/index.html` every time we run our `build` command).

Okay, we're all set up to deploy. Let's make an `npm` script to make our lives easier.

Every time we deploy, we'll want to rerun our `build` command to ensure that we have the freshest build of our project. Our `npm` script will thus combine both, added into our `package.json`:

```
"scripts": {
  "build": "node scripts/copy_assets.js &&
```

```
        node_modules/.bin/webpack --config webpack.config.prod.js",
          "start": "node_modules/.bin/webpack-dev-server",
          "deploy": "npm run build && firebase deploy"
        },
```

Run the script with `yarn deploy`, and then check out the URL it displays in the Terminal. If all goes well, your app should look exactly like it does in development. Open up the console and check for warnings; if you see any, skim the Webpack chapter and see whether you missed any of the settings for our `webpack.config.prod.js` (you can take a peek at the final file in the branch here: `https://github.com/scottdomes/chatastrophe/tree/chapter4`):

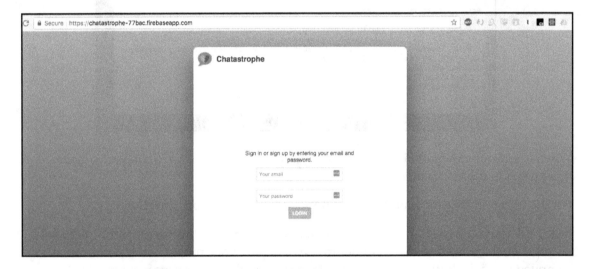

Awesome! We have a deployed app ready to share with our friends. The only problem is what we discussed at the end of the last chapter; it doesn't actually do much yet.

Let's get started with using Firebase by adding an authentication process.

# Authentication with Firebase

To allow users to log in/sign up for our app, we need to do three things:

1. Turn on email authentication on the Firebase console.
2. Submit the email and password in our form to Firebase when the user clicks on the button.
3. Either sign up or log in the user based on the result.

Let's open up our Firebase console (`https://console.firebase.google.com`) and get to work on task #1:

1. From our Chatastrophe project page, click on **Authentication**.
2. Under the **SIGN-IN METHOD** tab, you can see all the options that Firebase provides. These authentication solutions are huge boons to developers, as configuring authentication can be tricky (especially when working with third-party APIs, such as Twitter or Facebook). There's a lot of infrastructure to create to provide the proper security. Firebase takes care of that for us, so all we have to worry about is tapping into their system.
3. Click on **Email/Password** and then on **Enable** and **Save**. Our app can now use email and password combinations to sign up and log in. If you're looking to spice up our app a bit down the line, try implementing a Facebook or GitHub sign-in.

Get back to the app, and hop on over to `LoginContainer.js`. At the moment, when the user submits our form, we just prevent the default submission and log out our state:

```
handleSubmit = (event) => {
  event.preventDefault();
  console.log(this.state);
};
```

For our process, we will combine the signup and login processes into one. First, we'll check whether the email and password fields are filled in. If so, we'll try logging the user in, and if Firebase tells us that no user exists with that email, we'll create the user and sign them in automatically.

However, if the user does exist and we get a wrong password error, we'll alert the user by implementing a bit more state in our component.

Here's the plan:

```
handleSubmit = (event) => {
 event.preventDefault();
 // Step 1. Check if user filled out fields
 // Step 2. If yes, try to log them in.
 // Step 3. If login fails, sign them up.
 }
```

Firstly, check whether the fields are filled in:

```
handleSubmit = (event) => {
  event.preventDefault();
  if (this.state.email && this.state.password) {
    // Try to log them in.
  } else {
    // Display an error reminding them to fill out fields.
  }
}
```

Right away, we need a way to display an error to the user to tell them that they missed a field. Let's add an error string to our state:

```
state = { email: '', password: '', error: " }
```

We'll reset that error to an empty string every time they submit the form, but if they missed a field, we'll display the following text:

```
handleSubmit = (event) => {
  event.preventDefault();
  this.setState({ error: '' });
  if (this.state.email && this.state.password) {
    // Try to log them in.
  } else {
    this.setState({ error: 'Please fill in both fields.' });
  }
}
```

Lastly, to display the error, we'll add a `<p>` tag above our button, with the `className` of the error:

```
<input
  type="password"
  onChange={this.handlePasswordChange}
  value={this.state.password}
  placeholder="Your password" />
<p className="error">{this.state.error}</p>
<button className="red light" type="submit">Login</button>
```

Okay, try submitting our form without a field filled in. You can do so by either running the app locally (with your Dev server) or redeploying your changes. You should see the following:

It's looking good so far. The next step is to try to log the user in. At this point, our app has no users, so Firebase should return an error. Let's call Firebase with our email and password, and then console log the result.

The method we want to use is `firebase.auth().signInWithEmailAndPassword(email, password)`. This function returns a JavaScript promise. For those familiar with promises, you can skip to the next section, but it's worth brushing up on if you're unsure.

# What is a promise?

The problem with JavaScript is that it often deals with asynchronous operations. These are steps that the code must complete which don't follow a linear flow in time. Normally, code runs line by line, one after the other, but what happens when we need to call an API that takes a random number of seconds to respond? We can't just stop our code and wait, and we will still have certain lines of code to execute once that call is complete, whenever that is.

The solution used to be **callbacks**. If we were using `firebase.auth().signInWithEmailAndPassword` in this manner, it would look like this:

```
firebase.auth().signInWithEmailAndPassword(email, password, function()
{
   // Do something when the sign in is complete.
});
```

We would pass it a callback that is called when the operation is complete. This approach works fine, but can lead to some ugly code: specifically, something called the **pyramid of doom**, or **callback hell**, where nested callbacks lead to sloping code:

```
firebase.auth().signInWithEmailAndPassword(email, password, function()
{
  onLoginComplete(email, password, function() {
    onLoginCompleteComplete('contrived example', function() {
      anotherFunction('an argument', function () {
        console.log('Help I'm in callback hell!');
      });
    });
  });
});
```

To make working with asynchronous functions easier and cleaner, the people behind JavaScript implemented promises. **Promises** have a simple syntax: pass one function to a .then statement to be called when the operation is a success, and another to a .catch statement when the operation is a failure:

```
firebase.auth().signInWithEmailAndPassword(email, password)
  .then(() => { // Do something on success })
  .catch(err => { // Do something on failure. })
```

Now, our code is nice and readable, and we know exactly what code will be run when the operation is complete.

# Back to authentication

Since we expect an error to be returned (since we haven't signed up with any email and password combination), we can leave our then statement blank, but add a console log to our catch statement:

```
handleSubmit = (event) => {
  event.preventDefault();
  this.setState({ error: '' });
  if (this.state.email && this.state.password) {
    firebase.auth().signInWithEmailAndPassword(this.state.email,
this.state.password)
      .then(res => { console.log(res); })
      .catch(err => { console.log(err); })
  } else {
    this.setState({ error: 'Please fill in both fields.' });
  }
}
```

Submit your form, and you should be returned the following error:

```
{code: "auth/user-not-found", message: "There is no user record
corresponding to this identifier. The user may have been deleted."}
```

Great! This is exactly the error we wanted. This is the code we'll check for, before initiating the signup process. For now, we'll assume that all the other errors are due to an incorrect password:

```
handleSubmit = (event) => {
  event.preventDefault();
  this.setState({ error: '' });
  if (this.state.email && this.state.password) {
    firebase.auth().signInWithEmailAndPassword(this.state.email,
    this.state.password)
      .then(res => { console.log(res); })
      .catch(err => {
        if (error.code === 'auth/user-not-found') {
          // Sign up here.
        } else {
          this.setState({ error: 'Error logging in.' }) ;
        }
      })
  } else {
    this.setState({ error: 'Please fill in both fields.' });
  }
}
```

# Code cleanup

Our `handleSubmit` function is getting a little long and difficult to follow. Let's do some reorganization before we move on.

We'll start by moving everything after the initial `if` statement inside a separate function, called `login()`, for simplicity:

```
login() {
  firebase
    .auth()
    .signInWithEmailAndPassword(this.state.email, this.state.password)
    .then(res => {
      console.log(res);
    })
    .catch(err => {
      if (err.code === 'auth/user-not-found') {
        this.signup();
```

```
        } else {
          this.setState({ error: 'Error logging in.' });
        }
      });
    }
```

Then, our `handleSubmit` becomes much smaller:

```
handleSubmit = event => {
  event.preventDefault();
  this.setState({ error: '' });
  if (this.state.email && this.state.password) {
    this.login();
  } else {
    this.setState({ error: 'Please fill in both fields.' });
  }
};
```

It's much easier to read and follow now.

# Signing up

Let's get that signup process going. Again, it's a rather simple function name--
`firebase.auth().createUserWithEmailAndPassword(email, password)`. Again, it
returns a promise. Let's add `then` and `catch`, but leave the `then` as a console log for now:

```
signup() {
  firebase
    .auth()
    .createUserWithEmailAndPassword(this.state.email,
this.state.password)
    .then(res => {
      console.log(res);
    })
    .catch(error => {
      console.log(error);
      this.setState({ error: 'Error signing up.' });
    });
}
```

Try logging in to our app, and you should see a complicated user object show up in the
console. Success! We created our first user account. If you try logging in again with the
same account, you should see the same user object logged to the console.

You can try again with a different email and password combination (it doesn't matter if it's
a real email, for our purposes), and it should work smoothly.

# Saving our user

The `user` object we received in response to our `firebase.auth().signIn` seems like it'll be useful down the line. There may be numerous times we want access to the email of the currently signed-in user. Let's go ahead and save that in the state of our `App` component so that we can then pass it down to any `Container` component (once we make more containers).

There are two possible approaches: we can pass up the user object from `LoginContainer` to `App` via a callback through props, and `App` will pass a `handleLogin` function to `LoginContainer` as a prop, which will be called when the user logs in and sets the state of `App` appropriately.

Firebase gives us another option, however. As we discussed earlier, the Firebase database is real-time, which means changes to the data are automatically pushed to the frontend. All we need to do is set up the appropriate listener functions to wait for that change and act on it.

# Event listeners

**Event listeners** in JavaScript essentially work like so: we define an event and a callback we want to run when that event occurs. We can thus declare a function early on in our code, and only have it triggered later, whenever the specified event occurs.

Here's an example of listening for a resize of the browser window:

```
window.addEventListener('resize', function() { // Do something about
resize });
```

Firebase provides us with a function called `firebase.auth().onAuthStateChanged`. This function takes a callback as an argument, which is then called with the user object; it's perfect for our purposes!

The challenge, however, is when to declare this function in our `App` component. We want it to do the following:

```
firebase.auth().onAuthStateChanged((user) => {
  // If there is a user, save it to state.
  // If there is no user, do nothing.
});
```

However, this leads to a couple of restrictions:

- We only want to register the listener once, so we can't put it in the `render` method (which can be called multiple times as React updates the DOM)
- We need the `App` component to be fully loaded before registering the listener, because React complains if you try to `setState` on a non-existent component

In other words, we need to declare `onAuthStateChanged` at a particular time, that is, as soon as possible after `App` has appeared on the screen.

# Lifecycle methods

Fortunately, situations like this one are common in React, so the library provides us with a solution: a suite of functions called **lifecycle methods**. These methods come standard with all (class-based) React components, and are called at certain points as the component appears, updates, and disappears.

The lifecycle of a React component is as follows:

- The application has started, and the component's `render` method is about to be called
- The component has rendered and has now appeared on the screen
- The component is about to receive new props
- The component has received new props, and is about to call render again to update in response
- The component has updated in response to new props or a state change
- The component is about to disappear from the screen

Note that all of these don't necessarily occur with every component, but they are all quite common as our UI updates and changes.

The corresponding lifecycle methods are as listed:

- `componentWillMount`
- `componentDidMount`
- `componentWillReceiveProps`
- `componentWillUpdate`
- `componentDidUpdate`
- `componentWillUnmount`

Based on the preceding description, take a moment and try to figure out which lifecycle method we want to use to register our `onAuthStateChanged`.

Again, the point of time we're looking for is right after the component is first rendered. This makes `componentDidMount` the perfect choice; let's add it to our `App` component. We also need to initialize our state with the `user` key, which we'll work with in a second:

```
class App extends Component {
  state = { user: null };

  componentDidMount() {

  }

  render() {
    return (
      <div id="container">
        <LoginContainer />
      </div>
    );
  }
}
```

If you're unclear on lifecycle methods, try adding all six of them to your app with console logs in each one (as well as a `console.log` in the `render` method), and watch the lifecycle of your React component.

Okay, we can add `onAuthStateChanged` next:

```
componentDidMount() {
  firebase.auth().onAuthStateChanged((user) => {
    if (user) {
      this.setState({ user });
    }
  });
}
```

> Confused about the `this.setState({ user })`? That's called the ES6 property shorthand. Basically, when you're assigned a key to a variable, and the key and the variable should have the same name, you can save time instead of typing `this.setState({ user: user })`.

Note the `if` statement. `onAuthStateChanged` is also called when the user logs out, in which case the user argument will be null. We can set `this.state.user` to null, but let's keep it simple and let the user persist in state until the next user comes along.

Another bonus to Firebase authentication is that it takes care of persistent login for us. This means that a user won't have to log in every time they come to our app; Firebase will load their logged-in state automatically, until they click on sign out (which we'll add in the future). In accordance with this, `onAuthStateChanged` will be called every time that a user visits our app, whether they physically log in or are already logged in. Therefore, we can rely on our user object always being saved in state if the user is logged in.

You can try it by logging out the user in the callback of `onAuthStateChanged` with `firebase.auth().signOut();`. Try logging in again, and then refreshing the page; you should see the user object appear no matter how many times you refresh, as you are automatically logged in.

# Summary

That does it for authentication! Now, our users can log in to our app. The next step is to give them something to do once they sign in. For that, we need more pages, which leads us to our next topic: routing with React. How do we navigate between React components? How do we change the content of our app in accordance with the URL? All that and more is coming up next!

# 5
# Routing with React

"We've expanded the feature list."

You suppress a groan and wait.

"We want to give our users everything. Everything they need, everything they want, everything they could possibly ever desire."

"Okay," you say. "But this is a prototype…"

"A page for analytics, a page for their profile, a page for their friend's analytics, a page for taking notes, a page for the weather."

You quietly show yourself out, repeating under your breath, "It's a prototype."

## The plan

We've now arrived at the point where our application is technically working (in that we allow users to log in) but is lacking in real, useful content. It's time to change that.

To do so, however, we need to add additional pages to our application. Some of you may have heard the term **Single-Page Application** (**SPA**), which is used to refer to React apps and therefore may be confused by this talk of more pages. We'll cover that distinction as we move further on, and then move into our actual routing setup using React Router.

Here's what we'll learn:

- How to install and use React Router v4
- How to add additional routes to additional components
- How to move between routes

# Pages on pages

Luckily, saner heads prevail and the head product designer (the highest ranked of the five designers now employed by the company) says that they need only three views for the prototype: the login view (done!), the main chat view, and the user profile view.

Still, we clearly need a robust and extensible way to move between different screens in our app. We need a good solid routing solution.

Traditionally, routing has been a question of which HTML/CSS/JavaScript files are served up. You hit the URL at `static-site.com` and get the main `index.html`, then go to `static-site.com/resources` and get the `resources.html`.

In this model, the server gets a request for a certain URL and returns the appropriate files.

Increasingly, however, routing is moving to the client side. In a React world, we only ever serve up our `index.html` and `bundle.js`. Our JavaScript takes in the URL from the browser and then decides what JSX to render.

Hence the term Single-Page App--our user technically only ever sits on one page (if we look at it from the traditional model). However, they're able to navigate between other views, and do so in a much more streamlined way, without having to request more files from the server.

Our top-level container component (`App.js`) will always be rendered, but what changes is what is rendered inside it.

# The React Router difference

For some React routing solutions, the model will look something like the following.

We will render our initial screen, as shown:

```
<App>
  <LoginContainer />
</App>
```

This will fit with the URL of chatastrophe.com/login. When the user completes the login, we will send them to chatastrophe.com/chat. At that point, we will call ReactDOM.render with the following:

```
<App>
  <ChatContainer />
</App>
```

React's reconciliation engine will then compare the old app with the new app and swap out the components that have changes; in this case, it will swap LoginContainer for ChatContainer, without rerendering App.

Here's a very simple example of what that may look like, using a basic routing solution called page.js:

```
page('/', () => {
  ReactDOM.render(
    <App>
      <ChatContainer />
    </App>.
    document.getElementById('root')
  );
});

page('/login', () => {
 ReactDOM.render(
    <App>
     <LoginContainer />
    </App>.
    document.getElementById('root')
  );
});
```

This solution works fine. We're able to navigate between multiple views, and React's reconciliation ensures that there's no wasteful rerendering of unchanged components.

However, this solution is not very React-y. We're passing our entire application to ReactDOM.render each time we change the page, which leads to lots of repeated code in our router.js file. We're defining multiple versions of our application, rather than choosing precisely which components should render at which time.

In other words, this solution imposes a holistic approach to routing, rather than one split up by components.

Enter `React Router v4`, a complete rewrite of the library, which used to be a more traditional routing solution. The difference is that routes are now components that render based on the URL.

Let's talk about what that means exactly by rewriting our earlier example:

```
ReactDOM.render(
  <Router>
    <App>
      <Route path="/" component={ChatContainer} />
      <Route path="/login" component={LoginContainer} />
    </App>
  </Router>,
  document.getElementById('root')
);
```

Now, we only call `ReactDOM.render` once. We render our application, and within it, render two `Route` components wrapping our two containers.

Each `Route` takes a `path` prop. If the URL in the browser matches that `path`, the `Route` will render its child component (the container); otherwise, it will render nothing.

We never try to rerender our `App`. As it should be, it stays static. Furthermore, our routing solution is no longer kept separate from our components in a `router.js` file. Now, it lives within our components.

We can also nest our routes further within our components. Inside `LoginContainer`, we can add two routes--one for `/login`, and one for `/login/new`--if we wanted to have separate login and signup views.

In this model, every component can make a decision about what to render, based on the current URL.

I'll be honest, this approach is a bit weird to get used to, and I did not like it one bit when I started using it. For experienced developers, it requires thinking about your routing in a different way, rather than as a top-down, whole-page decision about what to render, you're now encouraged to make decisions at a component level, which can be difficult.

After some time working with it, however, I think this paradigm is exactly what's needed for a React approach to routing, and will give developers far more flexibility down the line.

Okay, enough talk. Let's create our second view--the chat screen--where users can view and send messages to everyone in the world at once ("global interconnectivity", you know). First, we'll create a basic component, and then we can get started with our routing solution.

# Our ChatContainer

Creating a component should be old news by now. Our `ChatContainer` will be a class-based component, since we'll need to tap into some lifecycle methods down the line (more on that later).

Inside our `components` folder, create a file called `ChatContainer.js`. Then, set up our skeleton:

```
import React, { Component } from 'react';

export default class ChatContainer extends Component {
  render() {
    return (

    );
  }
}
```

Let's continue our pattern of wrapping our component in a `div` with an `id` of the component name:

```
import React, { Component } from 'react';

export default class ChatContainer extends Component {
  render() {
    return (
      <div id="ChatContainer">
      </div>
    );
  }
}
```

Just as at the top of our `LoginContainer`, we will want to render our beautiful logo and title for our user to see. If only we had some sort of reuseable component so that we didn't have to rewrite that code:

```
import React, { Component } from 'react';
import Header from './Header';

export default class ChatContainer extends Component {
  render() {
    return (
      <div id="ChatContainer">
        <Header />
      </div>
    );
```

```
    }
  }
```

This is beautiful. Okay, let's just add `<h1>Hello from ChatContainer</h1>` after the `Header` and move on to routing so that we can actually see what we're doing as we work. Right now, our `ChatContainer` isn't visible. To change that, we need to set up React Router.

# Installing React Router

Let's start with the basics. Run the following in the Terminal from the project root.

```
yarn add react-router-dom@4.2.2
```

The `react-router-dom` contains all the React components we could want for routing our user through our application. You can view the full documentation for it at `https://reacttraining.com/react-router`. The only components we'll be interested in, however, are `Route` and `BrowserRouter`.

 It's important to ensure that you install `react-router-dom` and not `react-router`. Since version 4 was released, the package has been split into various branches. `React-router-dom` is specifically geared towards providing routing components, which is what we're interested in. Note that it installed `react-router` as a peer dependency, though.

The `Route` component is rather simple; it takes a prop called `path`, which is a string such as `/` or `/login`. When the URL in the browser matches that string (`http://chatastrophe.com/login`), the `Route` component renders the component, which is passed in via the `component` prop; otherwise, it renders nothing.

As with anything in web development, there's a lot of additional complexity to how you can use the `Route` component. We'll dive into it a bit more later on. For now, however, we only want to conditionally render either `ChatContainer` or `LoginContainer`, based on whether our path is `/` or `/login`.

`BrowserRouter` is more complicated, but for our purposes, it will be simple to use. Essentially, it ensures that our `Route` components are kept in sync (either rendering or not rendering) with the URL. It uses the HTML5 history API to do so.

# Our BrowserRouter

The first thing we need to do is wrap our entire application in the `BrowserRouter` component, then we can add our `Route` components.

Since we want to have our router around our entire application, the easiest place to add it is in our `src/index.js`. At the top, we require the following component:

```
import React from 'react';
import ReactDOM from 'react-dom';
import { BrowserRouter } from 'react-router-dom';
import App from './components/App';
```

Then, we render our `App` as a child of `BrowserRouter`:

```
ReactDOM.render(
  <BrowserRouter>
    <App />
  </BrowserRouter>,
  document.getElementById('root')
);
```

You should also do the same inside our hot re-loader configuration:

```
if (module.hot) {
  module.hot.accept('./components/App', () => {
    const NextApp = require('./components/App').default;
    ReactDOM.render(
      <BrowserRouter>
        <App />
      </BrowserRouter>,
      document.getElementById('root')
    );
  });
}
```

Done! Now we can actually start adding routes.

# Our first two Routes

Inside our `App` component, we currently render `LoginContainer`, no matter what:

```
render() {
  return (
    <div id="container">
```

```
        <LoginContainer />
      </div>
    );
  }
```

We want to change this logic so that we render either `LoginContainer` only or we render `ChatContainer`. To do that, let's require it in our `ChatContainer`.

We'll also require our `Route` component from `react-router-dom`:

```
import React, { Component } from 'react';
import { Route } from 'react-router-dom';
import LoginContainer from './LoginContainer';
import ChatContainer from './ChatContainer';
import './app.css';
```

 I put the `Route` import above the two `Container` imports. Best practices say you should put absolute imports (imports from `node_modules`) before relative imports (files imported from within `src`). This keeps things clean.

Now, we can replace our containers with `Route` components that take a `component` prop:

```
render() {
  return (
    <div id="container">
      <Route component={LoginContainer} />
      <Route component={ChatContainer} />
    </div>
  );
}
```

 We pass in our component prop as `LoginContainer`, and not as `<LoginContainer />`.

Our app reloads and we see... a mess:

We're currently rendering both containers at once! Oops. The problem is that we failed to give our `Route` a `path` prop that tells them when to render (and when not to). Let's do that now.

Our first `Route`, the `LoginContainer`, is to be rendered when we're at the `/login` route, so we add a path as follows:

```
<Route path="/login" component={LoginContainer} />
```

Our other container, `ChatContainer`, will be shown when the user is at the root, "/" (at `localhost:8080/` currently, or `https://chatastrophe-77bac.firebaseapp.com/` for our deployed app), so we add a path as shown:

```
<Route path="/" component={ChatContainer} />
```

Save, check the app, and you get the following:

Nice! Our `LoginContainer` no longer renders. Let's head over to `/login` and ensure that we only see our `LoginContainer` there:

Augh!

We're rendering both containers at `/login`. What happened?

Well, long story short, React Router uses a **RegEx** pattern to match routes and determine what to render. Our current path (`/login`) matches the prop passed to our login `Route`, but it also technically matches `/`. In fact, everything matches `/`, which is great if you have a component you want to render on every page, but we want our `ChatContainer` to only render when the path is `/` (with nothing else).

In other words, we want to render the `ChatContainer` route when the path is an exact match for `/`.

The good news is that React Router is prepared for this problem; simply add a prop `exact` to our `Route`:

```
<Route exact path="/" component={ChatContainer} />
```

 The preceding is the same as writing:
```
<Route exact={true} path="/" component={ChatContainer} />
```

When we check `/login`, we should only see our `LoginContainer`. Great! We have our first two routes.

The next thing we want to do is add a bit of forced routing; when the user logs in, we want to redirect them to the main chat screen. Let's do it!

# Redirecting on login

Here, things will get a bit more tricky. First, we'll do some preparation.

Inside our `LoginContainer`, when it comes to our `signup` and `login` methods, we currently just `console.log` out the result in our `then` statement. In other words, we don't actually do anything once our user logs in:

```
signup() {
  firebase.auth().createUserWithEmailAndPassword(this.state.email,
this.state.password)
    .then(res => {
      console.log(res);
    }).catch(error => {
      console.log(error);
      this.setState({ error: 'Error signing up.' });
    })
}
```

Let's change this bit (in both `signup` and `login`) to call another method, `onLogin`:

```
login() {
  firebase.auth().signInWithEmailAndPassword(this.state.email,
this.state.password)
    .then(res => {
```

```
    this.onLogin();
  }).catch((error) => {
    if (error.code === 'auth/user-not-found') {
      this.signup();
    } else {
      this.setState({ error: 'Error logging in.' });
    }
  });
}
```

Then, we can define our `onLogin` method:

```
onLogin() {
  // redirect to '/'
}
```

So, how do we redirect to the root path?

We know that our `Route` components will render based on the URL in the browser. We can be confident that if we modify the URL correctly, our app will rerender to display the appropriate component. The trick is to modify that URL from within `LoginContainer`.

As we mentioned earlier, React Router uses the HTML5 history API to move between URLs. In this model, there's an object called `history` with certain methods that allow you to push a new URL into the current state of the application.

So, if we're at `/login`, and want to go to `/`:

```
history.pushState(null, null, '/')
```

React Router lets us interact with the HTML5 history object in a more streamlined way (avoiding the null arguments, for example). The way it does so is simple: every component passed to a `Route` (via the `component` prop) receives another prop called `history`, which has a method called `push`.

If that sounds confusing, don't worry, it'll all be clear in a moment. All we have to do is this:

```
onLogin() {
  this.props.history.push('/');
}
```

Try it out by going to `/login` and logging in. You'll be redirected to the `ChatContainer`. Magic!

What's happening is the `history` prop, when `push` is called, is updating the browser's URL, which then causes our `Route` components to render their component (or render nothing):

```
History.push -> URL change -> Re-render
```

Note that this is a rather revolutionary way of navigating around a website. Previously, it was much different:

```
Click link/submit form -> URL change -> Download new page
```

Welcome to the world of routing single-page applications. Feels good, doesn't it?

# Logging out

Okay, we've handled our user logging in, but what about when they want to log out?

Let's build them a button at the top of `ChatContainer` to allow them to log out. It'll fit best in the `Header` component, so why don't we build it in there?

Well, hold up. We currently use the `Header` on our `/login` path, in the `LoginContainer`. If we add a `Logout` button, it'll appear on the sign-in screen as well, which is just confusing. We need a way to only render the `Logout` button on the `ChatContainer`.

We can take advantage of the `Route history` prop and use that to do a conditional rendering of the Logout button based on the URL (if the path is "/", render the button, otherwise don't!). However, that can be messy and hard to understand for future developers as we add more routes. Let's make it super explicit when we want the Logout button to appear.

In other words, we want to render the Logout button inside `Header`, but only when `Header` is inside `ChatContainer`. Does this make sense?

The way to do so is with React children. Children are actually super easy to understand, if you look at it from an HTML standpoint:

```html
<div>
  <h1>I am the child of div</h1>
</div>
```

h1 is the child of `div`. In the case of a React component the `Parent` component will receive a prop called `children`, which equals the h1 tag:

```
<Parent>
  <h1>I am the child of Parent</h1>
</Parent>
```

To render that within `Parent`, we just do this:

```
<div id="Parent">
  {this.props.children}
</div>
```

Let's see this in action and, hopefully, it'll make much more sense (and give you an idea of its power).

Inside `ChatContainer`, let's replace our `<Header />` tag with an opening and closing tag:

```
<Header>
</Header>
```

Inside that, we'll define our button:

```
<Header>
  <button className="red">Logout</button>
</Header>
```

Check our page and we see that nothing has changed. This is because we haven't told `Header` to actually render its `children`. Let's hop over to `Header.js` and change that.

Underneath our h1, add the following:

```
import React from 'react';

const Header = (props) => {
  return (
    <div id="Header">
      <img src="/assets/icon.png" alt="logo" />
      <h1>Chatastrophe</h1>
      {props.children}
    </div>
  );
};

export default Header;
```

What are we doing here? First, we're defining `props` as our argument to our functional component:

```
const Header = (props) => {
```

All functional React components receive the `props` object as their first argument.

Then, within that object, we're accessing the `children` property, which is equal to our button. Now, our `Logout` button should appear:

Awesome! If you check the `/login` path, you'll notice that our button does not appear. That's because in `LoginContainer`, `Header` has no `children`, so nothing is rendered.

 Children make React components super composable and extra reuseable.

Okay, let's make our button actually work. We want to call a method called `firebase.auth().signOut`. Let's make a click handler for our button that calls this function:

```
export default class ChatContainer extends Component {
  handleLogout = () => {
    firebase.auth().signOut();
  };
  render() {
    return (
      <div id="ChatContainer">
        <Header>
          <button className="red" onClick={this.handleLogout}>
            Logout
          </button>
        </Header>
        <h1>Hello from ChatContainer</h1>
      </div>
    );
  }
}
```

Now, when we press the button, nothing happens, but we are being logged out. We're missing one last piece of the login puzzle.

When our user logs out, we want to redirect them to the login screen. If only we had some way of telling the status of Firebase's authorization:

```
class App extends Component {
  componentDidMount() {
    firebase.auth().onAuthStateChanged((user) => {
      if (user) {
        this.setState({ user });
      }
    });
  }
}
```

This is perfect. After we click on the logout button, when our user logs out, Firebase will call `firebase.auth().onAuthStateChanged` with a null argument for the user. In other words, we already have everything we need; we just need to add an `else` to our `if` statement to cover situations where there is no user found.

The flow will go like this:

1. When the user clicks on the logout button, Firebase will log them out.
2. It will then call the `onAuthStateChanged` method with a null argument.
3. If `onAuthStateChanged` is called with a null user, we will redirect the user to the login page using the `history` prop.

Let's put this in place by jumping over to `App.js`.

Our `App` isn't the child of a `Route`, so it doesn't get access to the `history` prop that we used in `LoginContainer`, but there's a little workaround we can use.

At the top of `App.js`, add the following to our `react-router-dom` import:

```
import { Route, withRouter } from 'react-router-dom';
```

Then, at the bottom, replace our `export default` statement with this:

```
export default withRouter(App);
```

What's happening here? Essentially, `withRouter` is a function that takes a component as an argument and returns that component exactly as it was, except that now it has access to the `history` prop. We'll cover more on that as we move on, but let's finish this logout flow first.

Lastly, we can fill out `componentDidMount`:

```
componentDidMount() {
  firebase.auth().onAuthStateChanged((user) => {
    if (user) {
      this.setState({ user });
    } else {
      this.props.history.push('/login')
    }
  });
}
```

Try logging in again and hitting the logout button. You should be taken directly to the login screen. Magic!

# Detour - higher order components

In the preceding code, we used the `withRouter` function (imported from `react-router-dom`) to give our `App` component access to the `history` prop. Let's take a moment to talk about how that worked, since it's one of the most powerful React patterns you can learn.

`withRouter` is an example of a **Higher Order Component** (**HOC**). This slightly grandiose name is better than my favorite explanation: *Functions That Build Functions* (thanks to *Tom Coleman* for that one). Let's see an example.

Let's say that you had a `Button` component, as follows:

```
const Button = (props) => {
  return (
    <button style={props.style}>{props.text}</button>
  );
};
```

Also, let's say that we had a situation where we wanted it to have white text and a red background:

```
<Button style={{ backgroundColor: 'red', color: 'white' }} text="I am red!"
/>
```

As your app evolves, you're finding that you're using this particular styling a lot with this button. You need a lot of red buttons, with different text, and it's getting tiresome to type out `backgroundColor` every time.

Not only that; you also have another component, an alert box, with the same styles:

```
<AlertBox style={{ backgroundColor: 'red', color: 'white' }}
warning="ALERT!" />
```

Here, you have two options. You want two new components (`RedAlertBox` and `RedButton`), which you can use everywhere. You can define them as illustrated:

```
const RedButton = (props) => {
  return (
    <Button style={{ backgroundColor: 'red', color: 'white' }}
text={props.text} />
  );
};
```

And:

```
const RedAlertBox = (props) => {
  return (
    <AlertBox style={{ backgroundColor: 'red', color: 'white' }}
warning={props.text} />
  );
};
```

However, there's a simpler, more composable way, and that's to make a Higher Order Component.

What we want to achieve is a way to take a component and give it the red-on-white styling. That's it. We want to inject those props into any given component.

Let's look at the end result, and then what our HOC will look like. If we successfully make a HOC called `makeRed`, we can use it, as follows, to create our `RedButton` and `RedAlertBox`:

```
// RedButton.js
import Button from './Button'
import makeRed from './makeRed'

export default makeRed(Button)

// RedAlertBox.js
import AlertBox from './AlertBox'
import makeRed from './makeRed'

export default makeRed(AlertBox)
```

This is much easier, and much more reuseable. We can now reuse `makeRed` to convert any component into a nice red background and white text. That's power.

Okay, so how do we create a `makeRed` function? We want to take a component as an argument, and return that component with all its assigned props and the correct style prop:

```
import React from 'react';

const makeRed = (Component) => {
  const wrappedComponent = (props) => {
    return (
      <Component style={{ backgroundColor: 'red', color: 'white' }}
{...props} />
    );
  };
  return wrappedComponent;
}

export default makeRed;
```

Here's the same code, with comments:

```
import React from 'react';

// We receive a component constructor as an argument
const makeRed = (Component) => {
  // We make a new component constructor that takes props, just as any
component
  const wrappedComponent = (props) => {
    // This new component returns the original component, but with the
  style applied
    return (
      // But we also use the ES6 spread operator to apply the regular props
passed in.
      // The spread operator applies props like the text in <RedButton
text="hello" />
        to our new component
      // It will "spread" any and all props across our component
      <Component style={{ backgroundColor: 'red', color: 'white' }}
{...props} />
    );
  };
  // We return the new constructor, so it can be called as <RedButton /> or
<RedAlertBox />
  return wrappedComponent;
}

export default makeRed;
```

The most confusing thing will likely be the spread operator of {...props}. The spread operator is a useful yet confusing ES6 tool. It allows you to take an object (here, the props object) and apply all its keys and values to a new object (the component):

```
const obj1 = { 1: 'one', 2: 'two' };
const obj2 = { 3: 'three', ...obj1 };
console.log(obj2);
// { 1: 'one', 2: 'two', 3: 'three' }
```

Higher order components are a next-level tool to make your React components easier to reuse. We've only scratched their surface here. For more information, check out *Understanding Higher Order Components* by *Tom Coleman*, at https://medium.freecodecamp. org/understanding-higher-order-components-6ce359d761b.

# Our third Route

As discussed at the beginning of this chapter, the Chatastrophe team is set on having a user profile view. Let's do the skeleton and basic routing for that.

In src/components, make a new file called UserContainer.js. Inside, do the basic component skeleton:

```
import React, { Component } from 'react';
import Header from './Header';

export default class UserContainer extends Component {
  render() {
    return (
      <div id="UserContainer">
        <Header />
        <h1>Hello from UserContainer</h1>
      </div>
    );
  }
}
```

Back in App.js, let's import our new container and add the Route component:

```
import UserContainer from './UserContainer';

// Inside render, underneath ChatContainer Route
<Route path="/users" component={UserContainer} />
```

Hold on! The preceding code creates a route at /users for our UserContainer, but we don't have just one user view. We have a user view for every user of our application. We need to have a route for User 1 at chatastrophe.com/users/1, and for User 2 at chatastrophe.com/users/2, and so on.

We need some way to pass a variable value to our path prop, equal to the user id. Fortunately, it's easy to do so:

```
<Route path="/users/:id" component={UserContainer} />
```

The best part? Now, in our UserContainer, we'll receive a props.params.match object, equal to { id: 1 } or whatever the id is, which we can then use to fetch that user's messages.

Let's test that by changing our h1 in UserContainer.js:

```
<h1>Hello from UserContainer for User {this.props.match.params.id}</h1>
```

Then, head to localhost:8080/users/1:

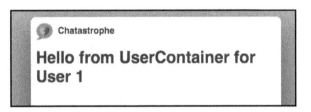

If you run into problems with finding bundle.js when in a nested route, ensure that your output inside your webpack.config.js looks like this:

```
output: {
  path: __dirname + "/public",
  filename: "bundle.js",
  publicPath: "/"
},
```

Beautiful. Now, there's one last step. Let's add a way for the user to return to the main chat screen from the UserContainer.

We can do so in a really easy way by taking advantage of the `Header` children again; only, in this case, we can add in another React Router component to make our lives super easy. It's called `Link`, and it's just like a tag in HTML, but is optimized for React Router.

In `UserContainer.js`:

```
import { Link } from 'react-router-dom';

<Header>
  <Link to="/">
    <button className="red">
      Back To Chat
    </button>
  </Link>
</Header>
```

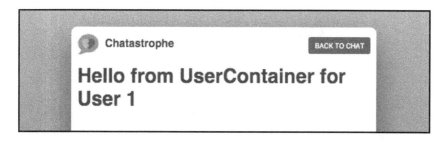

When you click on the button, you should be taken to the root route of `/`.

# Summary

That's it! We covered a lot in this chapter in order to get our application's routing solution up and running. If anything is confusing, I invite you to take a look at the React Router docs at `https://reacttraining.com/react-router/`. Next, we'll go much, much deeper into React, as we finish up our basic application, and then start converting it into a Progressive Web App.

# 6
# Completing Our App

It's time to finish up the prototype of our application, and boy, do we have our work cut out for us.

The skeleton is in place, with all our routes set up and our login screen fully complete. However, our chat and user views are blank as of yet, and that's where the core functionality of Chatastrophe will live. So, before we show our prototype to the board, let's make it actually, uh, work.

What we'll be covering this chapter is as listed:

- Loading and displaying chat messages
- Sending and receiving new messages
- Displaying only certain chat messages on the user profile page
- React state management

## User stories progress

Let's briefly check in with the user stories we defined in Chapter 1, *Creating Our App Structure*, and see which ones we have already accomplished.

We've completed the following:

Users should be able to log in and out of the application.

The following are unfinished, but are part of the PWA functionality we'll build later:

- Users should be able to view their messages even when offline
- Users should receive push notifications when a message is sent by another user
- Users should be able to install the app to their mobile device
- Users should be able to load the app in under five seconds, even under shaky network conditions

That leaves us with a list of stories we need to complete before our prototype is complete:

- Users should be able to send and receive messages in real time
- Users should be able to view all messages by a given author

Each of these stories fit with a certain view (Chat view and User view). Let's start with the ChatContainer, and begin building out our chat box.

# ChatContainer skeleton

Our chat view will have two main sections:

- A message display where all chats are listed
- A chat box for the user to type in a new message

We can start by adding the appropriate div tags:

```
render() {
  return (
    <div id="ChatContainer">
      <Header>
        <button className="red" onClick={this.handleLogout}>
          Logout
        </button>
      </Header>
      <div id="message-container">
      </div>
      <div id="chat-input">
      </div>
    </div>
  );
}
```

Reminder to ensure that your IDs and classNames are the same as mine, lest your CSS be different (or even worse).

We'll fill in the input box first. Inside `div#chat-input`, let's place a `textarea`, with a placeholder of `"Add your message..."`:

```
<textarea placeholder="Add your message..." />
```

We will configure it to allow the user to press *Enter* to send a message, but it's better to also have a **Send** button. Below the `textarea`, add a `button`, and inside that, we'll add an SVG icon:

```
<div id="chat-input">
  <textarea placeholder="Add your message..." />
  <button>
    <svg viewBox="0 0 24 24">
      <path fill="#424242" d="M2,21L23,12L2,3V10L17,12L2,14V21Z" />
    </svg>
  </button>
</div>
```

Ensure that your `path fill` and `svg viewBox` properties are the same as mentioned.

SVGs are a type of image that can be scaled (made larger) without any loss of quality. In this case, we're essentially creating a box (the `svg` tag) and then drawing a line within the `path` tag. The browser does the actual drawing, so there's never any pixelation.

Let's also give our `div#ChatContainer` the class of `inner-container` for CSS purposes:

```
<div id="ChatContainer" className="inner-container">
```

If all went well, your app should now look like this:

This does it for the basic structure of our chat view. Now, we can start discussing how we will manage our data--the list of messages coming in from Firebase.

# Managing data flow

One of the important principles of React is something called **uni-directional data flow**.

In the prototypical React app, data is stored in the state of the highest-level component, and passed **down** to lower-level components via `props`. When the user interacts with the application, the interaction event is passed **up** through the component tree via props, until it arrives at the highest-level component, which then modifies the state based on the action.

The application then forms a big circle--data goes down, events come up, and new data goes down. You can also think of it as an elevator, departing from the top floor full of data, and then coming back up full of events.

The advantage of this approach is that it's easy to follow the flow of data. You can see where it's going (to which child components), and why it's changing (in reaction to which events).

Now, this model runs into problems with a complex application with hundreds of components. It becomes unwieldy to store all your state in the top-level component, and pass all your data and events through props.

Think of a big chain from your top-level component (App.js) and a low-level component (say, a button). If there are dozens of nested components, and the button needs a prop that is derived from the state of App, you will have to pass that prop down through every single component in the chain. No thanks.

There are numerous solutions to this problem of state management, but most work on the idea of creating container components throughout the component tree; these components have state, and pass it down to a limited number of child components. Now we have multiple elevators, some serving the first to third floor, others the fifth to twelfth, and so on.

We won't be dealing with any state management in our application since we only have four components, but it's good to keep this in mind as your React app scales.

 The top two React state management libraries are Redux (https://github.com/reactjs/redux) and MobX (https://github.com/mobxjs/mobx). I've worked extensively with both, and both have their advantages and tradeoffs. In short, MobX is better for developer productivity, while Redux is better for keeping large applications organized.

For our purposes, we can store all our state in our App component, and pass it down to our child components. Rather than storing our messages in ChatContainer, we store them in App and pass them down to ChatContainer. This immediately gives us the advantage of also passing them down to UserContainer.

In other words, our messages live in the state of App, and are shared with UserContainer and ChatContainer via props.

State is the single source of truth in your application, and should never be duplicated. It won't make sense to store two message arrays: one in ChatContainer and one in UserContainer. Instead, store state as high as necessary, and pass it down.

Long story short, we need to load our messages in App, and then pass them down to ChatContainer. It also makes sense to put App in charge of sending the messages so that all our message functionality is in one place.

Let's start with sending our first message!

# Creating a message

As in our `LoginContainer`, we need to store the value of our `textarea` in state as it changes.

We used the state of the `LoginContainer` to store that value. Let's do the same with `ChatContainer`.

 You may be wondering, after the preceding discussion: why don't we just keep all our state in App? Some will argue for that approach, to keep everything in one place; however, this will bloat our App component and require us to pass multiple `props` between components. It's better to keep state as high as necessary, and no higher; the new message in the chat input will only be relevant to App when it's done and submitted, not before that.

Let's get that set up.

Add this to the `ChatContainer.js`:

```
state = { newMessage: '' };
```

Also, add a method to handle it:

```
handleInputChange = e => {
  this.setState({ newMessage: e.target.value });
};
```

Now, modify our `textarea`:

```
<textarea
    placeholder="Add your message..."
    onChange={this.handleInputChange}
    value={this.state.newMessage}
/>
```

 Best practices say that you should always make your JSX element multiline when it has more than two `props` (or the `props` are particularly long).

When our user clicks on **Send**, we want to send the message to `App`, which will then send it to Firebase. After that, we reset the field:

```
handleSubmit = () => {
    this.props.onSubmit(this.state.newMessage);
    this.setState({ newMessage: " });
};
```

We haven't added this `onSubmit` prop function yet in `App`, but we can do that soon:

```
<button onClick={this.handleSubmit}>
  <svg viewBox="0 0 24 24">
    <path fill="#424242" d="M2,21L23,12L2,3V10L17,12L2,14V21Z" />
  </svg>
</button>
```

However, we also want to let users submit by pressing *Enter*. How can we do so?

At the moment, we listen for the change event on the `textarea`, and then call the `handleInputChange` method. The prop on `textarea` that listens for changes in its value is `onChange`, but there's another event, key-down, which occurs whenever the user presses a key.

We can watch for that event and then check what key was pressed; if it's *Enter*, we send our message!

Let's see it in action:

```
<textarea
    placeholder="Add your message..."
    onChange={this.handleInputChange}
    onKeyDown={this.handleKeyDown}
    value={this.state.newMessage} />
```

The following is the handler for this event:

```
handleKeyDown = e => {
  if (e.key === 'Enter') {
    e.preventDefault();
    this.handleSubmit();
  }
}
```

The event handler (`handleKeyDown`) is called with an event passed in as the first argument automatically. This event has a property named `key`, which is a string indicating the value of the key. We also need to prevent the default behavior (creating a newline in the `textarea`) before submitting the message.

You can use this kind of event listener for all sorts of user inputs, from hovering over an element to shift-clicking something.

Before we move to App.js, here's the current state of ChatContainer:

```
import React, { Component } from 'react';
import Header from './Header';

export default class ChatContainer extends Component {
  state = { newMessage: '' };

  handleLogout = () => {
    firebase.auth().signOut();
  };

  handleInputChange = e => {
    this.setState({ newMessage: e.target.value });
  };

  handleSubmit = () => {
    this.props.onSubmit(this.state.newMessage);
    this.setState({ newMessage: '' });
  };

  handleKeyDown = e => {
    if (e.key === 'Enter') {
      e.preventDefault();
      this.handleSubmit();
    }
  };

  render() {
    return (
      <div id="ChatContainer" className="inner-container">
        <Header>
          <button className="red" onClick={this.handleLogout}>
            Logout
          </button>
        </Header>
        <div id="message-container" />
        <div id="chat-input">
          <textarea
            placeholder="Add your message..."
            onChange={this.handleInputChange}
            onKeyDown={this.handleKeyDown}
            value={this.state.newMessage}
          />
          <button onClick={this.handleSubmit}>
```

```
            <svg viewBox="0 0 24 24">
              <path fill="#424242" d="M2,21L23,12L2,3V10L17,12L2,14V21Z" />
            </svg>
          </button>
        </div>
      </div>
    );
  }
}
```

Okay, let's add the last link in the chain to create a message. In App.js, we need to add a handler for the onSubmit event, which we'll pass in as a prop to ChatContainer:

```
// in App.js
handleSubmitMessage = msg => {
  // Send to database
  console.log(msg);
};
```

We want to pass an onSubmit prop to ChatContainer that equals this method, but wait a second, our ChatContainer is currently rendered as follows:

```
<Route exact path="/" component={ChatContainer} />
```

ChatContainer itself is a prop on our Route. How can we give ChatContainer any props at all?

It turns out that the React Router provides three distinct methods of rendering components inside Route. The simplest way is the route (ha ha) we chose earlier, passing it in as a prop called component.

There's another, better way for our purposes--a prop called render, into which we pass a function that returns our component.

The third way to render a component inside Route is via a prop called children, which takes a function with a match argument, which is either defined or null, depending on whether the path prop matches the browser's URL. The JSX returned by the function is always rendered, but you can modify it based on the match argument.

Let's switch our Route over to this method:

```
<Route
  exact
  path="/"
  render={() => <ChatContainer onSubmit={this.handleSubmitMessage} />}
/>
```

The preceding example uses an ES6 arrow function with implicit return. This is the same as writing `() => { return <ChatContainer onSubmit={this.handleSubmitMessage} /> }` or, in ES5, `function() { return <ChatContainer onSubmit={this.handleSubmitMessage} /> }`.

Now, we can pass all the props we like to `ChatContainer`.

Let's ensure that it works. Try sending a message, and ensure that you see the `console.log` we added in `handleSubmit` in `App.js`.

If so, great! Time to move on to the good part--actually sending the message.

# Sending a message to Firebase

To write to the Firebase database, first we grab an instance of it, with `firebase.database()`. Similar to `firebase.auth()`, this instance comes with some built-in methods we can use.

The one we will be dealing with in this book is `firebase.database().ref(refName)`. `Ref` stands for **reference**, but might be better thought of as a category of our data (in SQL databases, what might make up a table).

If we want to grab the reference to our users, we use `firebase.database().ref('/users')`. For messages, it's `firebase.database().ref('/messages')` ... and so on. We can now act on this reference in a variety of ways, such as listening to changes (coming later in the chapter), or pushing new data in (which we'll handle right now).

To add new data to a reference, you use `firebase.database().ref('/messages').push(data)`. In this context, it is useful to think of the `ref` as a simple JavaScript array, which we're pushing new data into.

Firebase will take it from there, saving the data to the NoSQL database and pushing out a 'value' event to all instances of the application, which we'll tap into later.

# Our message data

We want to save the message text to the database, of course, but we also want to save a bit more information.

Our users need to be able to see who sent the message (preferably, an email address), and be able to navigate to their `users/:id` page. So, we need to save the email address of the author with the message as well as a unique user ID. Let's throw in a `timestamp` for good measure:

```
// App.js
handleSubmitMessage = msg => {
  const data = {
    msg,
    author: this.state.user.email,
    user_id: this.state.user.uid,
    timestamp: Date.now()
  };
  // Send to database
}
```

 The preceding example uses ES6's property shorthand for the message field. Instead of writing `{ msg: msg }`, we can simply write `{ msg }`.

Here, we're taking advantage of the fact that we saved the current user into the state of our App component, and grabbing the email and the uid (a unique ID) from it. Then, we create a `timestamp` with `Date.now()`.

Okay, let's send it off!:

```
handleSubmitMessage = (msg) => {
  const data = {
    msg,
    author: this.state.user.email,
    user_id: this.state.user.uid,
    timestamp: Date.now()
  };
  firebase
      .database()
      .ref('messages/')
      .push(data);
}
```

Before we test it, let's open our Firebase console at `console.firebase.google.com` and go to the database tab. Here, we can see a real-time representation of our database data, so we can check to ensure that our message is being created correctly.

As of now, it should look like this:

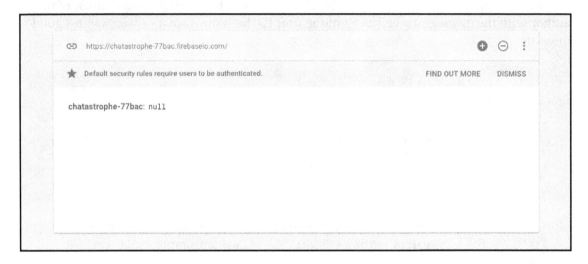

Let's type a message into our chat input, and press **Enter**.

You should see the following instantly appear on the Firebase console:

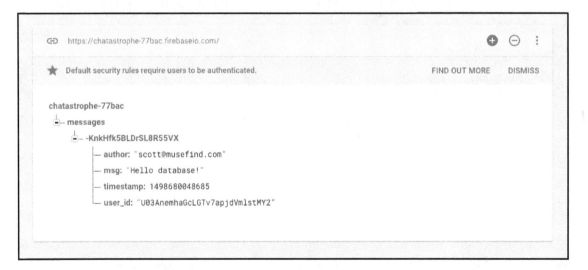

Great! We sent our first chat messages, but nothing appears in our app. Let's fix that.

# Loading data from Firebase

As we described earlier, we can listen for changes to a particular reference in our database. In other words, we can define a function to run every time `firebase.database().ref('/messages')` changes, as a new message comes in.

Before we move on, I'd encourage you to consider two things: where we should define this listener, and what the function should do.

See if you can come up with a possible implementation! After you've brainstormed an idea, let's build it.

Here's the thing: we already have a very similar case in our application. Our `firebase.auth().onAuthStateChanged` in our `App#componentDidMount` listens for changes in our current user, and updates the `state.user` of our `App`.

We will do the exact same thing with our messages reference, though the syntax is a bit different:

```
class App extends Component {
  state = { user: null, messages: [] }
  componentDidMount() {
    firebase.auth().onAuthStateChanged((user) => {
      if (user) {
        this.setState({ user });
      } else {
        this.props.history.push('/login')
      }
    });
    firebase
      .database()
      .ref('/messages')
      .on('value', snapshot => {
        console.log(snapshot);
      });
  }
```

We use the `.on` function to listen for a `'value'` event from the database. Our callback is then called with an argument called `snapshot`. Let's plug this in and send another message, and take a look at what our snapshot looks like:

```
▼ V {A: 0, V: U, g: rc}
  ▶ A: 0
  ▶ V: U
  ▶ g: rc
    key: (...)
    ref: (...)
  ▶ __proto__: Object
> |
```

Ah, it's not very developer friendly.

The snapshot is, somewhere in that object, an image of the database structure of `/messages`. We can access a more readable form by calling `val()` on it:

```
firebase.database().ref('/messages').on('value', snapshot => {
  console.log(snapshot.val());
});
```

```
▼ Object {-KnkHfk5BLDrSL8R55VX: Object, -KnkP-zWj0gv-uR6tJiy: Object, -KnkPU2heIlRYWXYltOs: Object}
  ▼ -KnkHfk5BLDrSL8R55VX: Object
      author: "scott@musefind.com"
      msg: "Hello database!"
      timestamp: 1498680048685
      user_id: "U03AnemhaGcLGTv7apjdVmlstMY2"
    ▶ __proto__: Object
  ▶ -KnkP-zWj0gv-uR6tJiy: Object
  ▶ -KnkPU2heIlRYWXYltOs: Object
  ▶ __proto__: Object
```

Now, we can get an object that contains each of our messages, with the message ID as the keys.

Here, we need to do some trickery. We want to update our `state.messages` with an array of our messages, but we want to add the message ID to the message object (since the message ID is currently the key in the `snapshot.val()`).

If this sounds confusing, hopefully it'll be clearer when we see it in action. We will create a new array called `messages`, and iterate over our object (using a method called `Object.keys`) and then push the message (with the ID) into the new array.

Let's extract this to a new function:

```
class App extends Component {
  state = { user: null, messages: [] }
  componentDidMount() {
    firebase.auth().onAuthStateChanged((user) => {
      if (user) {
        this.setState({ user });
      } else {
        this.props.history.push('/login')
      }
    });
    firebase
      .database()
      .ref('/messages')
      .on('value', snapshot => {
        this.onMessage(snapshot);
      });
  }
```

Also, the new method:

```
onMessage = snapshot => {
  const messages = Object.keys(snapshot.val()).map(key => {
    const msg = snapshot.val()[key];
    msg.id = key;
    return msg;
  });
  console.log(messages);
};
```

What we end up with, in our `console.log`, is a nice array of messages with IDs:

```
▼ (3) [Object, Object, Object]
  ▼ 0: Object
      author: "scott@musefind.com"
      id: "-KnkHfk5BLDrSL8R55VX"
      msg: "Hello database!"
      timestamp: 1498680048685
      user_id: "U03AnemhaGcLGTv7apjdVmlstMY2"
    ▶ __proto__: Object
  ▼ 1: Object
      author: "scott@musefind.com"
      id: "-KnkP-zWj0gv-uR6tJiy"
      msg: "Hello"
      timestamp: 1498681970012
      user_id: "U03AnemhaGcLGTv7apjdVmlstMY2"
    ▶ __proto__: Object
```

The last step is to save this to state:

```
onMessage = (snapshot) => {
  const messages = Object.keys(snapshot.val()).map(key => {
    const msg = snapshot.val()[key]
    msg.id = key
    return msg
  });
  this.setState({ messages });
}
```

Now, we can pass our messages down to `ChatContainer`, and get to work displaying them:

```
<Route
  exact
  path="/"
  render={() => (
    <ChatContainer
      onSubmit={this.handleSubmitMessage}
      messages={this.state.messages}
    />
  )}
/>
```

We've made a lot of changes to `App.js`. Here's the current code:

```
import React, { Component } from 'react';
import { Route, withRouter } from 'react-router-dom';
import LoginContainer from './LoginContainer';
import ChatContainer from './ChatContainer';
import UserContainer from './UserContainer';
import './app.css';

class App extends Component {
  state = { user: null, messages: [] };

  componentDidMount() {
    firebase.auth().onAuthStateChanged(user => {
      if (user) {
        this.setState({ user });
      } else {
        this.props.history.push('/login');
      }
    });
    firebase
      .database()
      .ref('/messages')
```

```
      .on('value', snapshot => {
        this.onMessage(snapshot);
      });
  }

  onMessage = snapshot => {
    const messages = Object.keys(snapshot.val()).map(key => {
      const msg = snapshot.val()[key];
      msg.id = key;
      return msg;
    });
    this.setState({ messages });
  };

  handleSubmitMessage = msg => {
    const data = {
      msg,
      author: this.state.user.email,
      user_id: this.state.user.uid,
      timestamp: Date.now()
    };
    firebase
      .database()
      .ref('messages/')
      .push(data);
  };

  render() {
    return (
      <div id="container">
        <Route path="/login" component={LoginContainer} />
        <Route
          exact
          path="/"
          render={() => (
            <ChatContainer
              onSubmit={this.handleSubmitMessage}
              messages={this.state.messages}
            />
          )}
        />
        <Route path="/users/:id" component={UserContainer} />
      </div>
    );
  }
}

export default withRouter(App);
```

# Displaying our messages

We will use the `Array.map()` function to iterate over our array of messages, and create an array of divs to display the data.

`Array.map()` automatically returns an array, which means we can embed that functionality right into our JSX. This is a common pattern in React (usually for displaying collections of data like this), so it's worth watching closely.

Inside our `message-container`, we create opening and closing squiggly brackets:

```
<div id="message-container">
  {
  }
</div>
```

Then, we call `map` on our message array, and pass in a function to create the new message `div`:

```
<div id="message-container">
  {this.props.messages.map(msg => (
    <div key={msg.id} className="message">
      <p>{msg.msg}</p>
    </div>
  ))}
</div>
```

If all goes well, you should see the following, with all the messages you've sent:

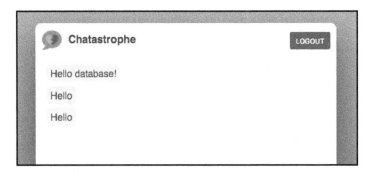

You can even try writing a new message, and watch it instantly appear in the message container. Magic!

A few notes about the preceding code:

- The `map` function goes over each element in the messages array, and creates a `div` based on its data. When it's done iterating, it returns that array of divs, which is then displayed as part of our JSX.
- One of the quirks of React is that each element on the screen needs a unique identifier so that React can update it properly. That's hard for React to do when dealing with a collection of the same elements, as we are creating here. Thus, we have to give each message div a key prop that is guaranteed to be unique.

 For more on lists and keys, visit `https://facebook.github.io/react/docs/lists-and-keys.html`.

Let's add a bit more functionality, and display the author name below the message, with a link to their user page. We can use the React Router `Link` component to do so; it's similar to an anchor tag (`<a>`), but is optimized for React Router:

```
import { Link } from 'react-router-dom';
```

Then, add it in the following:

```
<div id="message-container">
  {this.props.messages.map(msg => (
    <div key={msg.id} className="message">
      <p>{msg.msg}</p>
      <p className="author">
        <Link to={`/users/${msg.user_id}`}>{msg.author}</Link>
      </p>
    </div>
  ))}
</div>
```

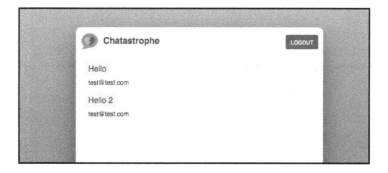

**TIP**

The `to` prop on the `Link` uses ES6 string interpolation. If you wrap your string in backticks (`) instead of quotation marks, you can use `${VARIABLE}` to embed variables right into it.

Now, we will make our messages look even better!

# Message display improvements

Let's take some time to do some quick UI improvements to our message display, before we move on to the user profile page.

## Multiple users

If you try logging out and signing in with a new user, all the messages from all users are displayed, as shown:

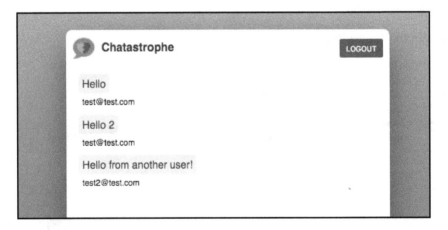

There's no differentiation between my messages, and the messages of other users. The classic chat application pattern is to put one user's messages on one side, and one on the other. Our CSS is all ready to handle that—we just have to assign the class "mine" to messages that match the current user.

Since we have access to the email of the message author in `msg.author`, we can compare that to the user we have stored in the state of `App`. Let's pass that down as a prop to `ChatContainer`:

```
<Route
  exact
  path="/"
  render={() => (
    <ChatContainer
      onSubmit={this.handleSubmitMessage}
      user={this.state.user}
      messages={this.state.messages}
    />
  )}
/>
```

Then, we can add a conditional in our `className` property:

```
<div id="message-container">
  {this.props.messages.map(msg => (
    <div
      key={msg.id}
      className={`message ${this.props.user.email === msg.author &&
        'mine'}`}>
      <p>{msg.msg}</p>
      <p className="author">
        <Link to={`/users/${msg.user_id}`}>{msg.author}</Link>
      </p>
    </div>
  ))}
</div>
```

This uses ES6 string interpolation along with short-circuit evaluation to create the effect we want. Those are the fancy terms for what boils down to this: if the message author matches the user email in `state`, set the `className` to `message mine`; otherwise, set it to `message`.

It should end up looking like this:

# Batching user messages

In the preceding screenshot, you'll notice that we display the author email under each message, even if two messages in the row have the same author. Let's get tricky, and make it so that we group messages from the same author together.

In other words, we only want to display the author email if the next message is not by the same author:

```
<div id="message-container">
  {this.props.messages.map(msg => (
    <div
      key={msg.id}
      className={`message ${this.props.user.email === msg.author &&
        'mine'}`}>
      <p>{msg.msg}</p>
      // Only if the next message's author is NOT the same as this
message's    author, return the following:
      <p className="author">
        <Link to={`/users/${msg.user_id}`}>{msg.author}</Link>
      </p>
    </div>
  ))}
</div>
```

How can we do this? We need a way to check the next message in the array, from the current message.

Luckily, the `Array.map()` function passes the index to our callback as the second element. We can use it, as illustrated:

```
<div id="message-container">
  {this.props.messages.map((msg, i) => (
    <div
      key={msg.id}
      className={`message ${this.props.user.email === msg.author &&
        'mine'}`}>
      <p>{msg.msg}</p>
      {(!this.props.messages[i + 1] ||
        this.props.messages[i + 1].author !== msg.author) && (
        <p className="author">
          <Link to={`/users/${msg.user_id}`}>{msg.author}</Link>
        </p>
      )}
    </div>
  ))}
</div>
```

Now, we're saying: "If there is a next message, and the next message's author is not the same as the current message's author, show the author for this message."

However, this is a lot of complex logic in our `render` method. Let's extract it to a method:

```
<div id="message-container">
  {this.props.messages.map((msg, i) => (
    <div
      key={msg.id}
      className={`message ${this.props.user.email === msg.author &&
        'mine'}`}>
      <p>{msg.msg}</p>
      {this.getAuthor(msg, this.props.messages[i + 1])}
    </div>
  ))}
</div>
```

Also, the method itself:

```
getAuthor = (msg, nextMsg) => {
  if (!nextMsg || nextMsg.author !== msg.author) {
    return (
      <p className="author">
        <Link to={`/users/${msg.user_id}`}>{msg.author}</Link>
      </p>
    );
  }
};
```

Our messages are now grouped like this:

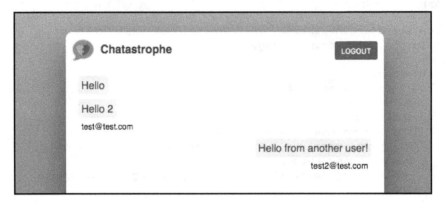

# Scrolling down

Try making your browser smaller so that your list of messages is almost cut off; then, submit another message. Note that you have to scroll down to see it, if it's past the cut off of the message container. This is bad UX. Let's make it so that we automatically scroll down when a new message arrives.

In this section, we will dive into two powerful React concepts: the `componentDidUpdate` method, and refs.

Let's start by discussing what we want to achieve. We want our message container to be scrolled down to the bottom so that the most recent messages are always in view (unless the user decides to scroll up to see older messages). This means we need the message container to scroll down in two situations:

- When the first component is rendered
- When new messages arrive

Let's start with the first use case. We will need a React life cycle method--one we've already used. We will add a `componentDidMount` method to our `ChatContainer`, just like we did with `App`.

Let's define it, and a `scrollToBottom` method as well:

```
export default class ChatContainer extends Component {
  state = { newMessage: '' };

  componentDidMount() {
```

```
    this.scrollToBottom();
  }

  scrollToBottom = () => {

  };
```

We also want to trigger the `scrollToBottom` method whenever new messages arrive, have appeared on the screen. React gives us another method to deal with this situation-- `componentDidUpdate`. This method is called whenever your React component updates due to new `props` or state. The best part is that the method gets the previous `props` passed as the first argument, so we can compare them and find the difference, as follows:

```
componentDidUpdate(previousProps) {
  if (previousProps.messages.length !== this.props.messages.length) {
    this.scrollToBottom();
  }
}
```

We look at the length of the messages array in the previous `props`, and compare it to the length of the messages array in the current `props`. If it has changed, we scroll to the bottom.

Okay, all that looks good. Let's go ahead and get our `scrollToBottom` method working.

# React refs

Refs in React are a way to grab a particular DOM element. For those familiar with jQuery, refs bridge the gap between the React approach of creating elements with props and the jQuery approach of grabbing things from the DOM and manipulating them.

We can add a `ref` to any JSX element we want to use later (that we want to refer to later). Let's add one to our message container. The `ref` prop is always a function, which is called with the element in question, and then used to assign that element to a property of the component, as shown:

```
<div
  id="message-container"
  ref={element => {
    this.messageContainer = element;
  }}>
```

Inside our `scrollToBottom` method, we use `ReactDOM.findDOMNode` to grab the element in question (don't forget to import react-dom!):

```
import ReactDOM from 'react-dom';

scrollToBottom = () => {
  const messageContainer = ReactDOM.findDOMNode(this.messageContainer);
}
```

In the next section, we will make it such that we only show our message container when the messages are loaded. For that reason, we need an `if` statement to check whether our `messageContainer` DOM node currently exists. Once that is done, we can set the `messageContainer.scrollTop` (how far it is currently scrolled down) to its height so that it's at the bottom:

```
scrollToBottom = () => {
  const messageContainer = ReactDOM.findDOMNode(this.messageContainer);
  if (messageContainer) {
    messageContainer.scrollTop = messageContainer.scrollHeight;
  }
}
```

Now if you try reducing the size of your browser and sending a message, you should always be taken to the bottom of the message container so that it's automatically in view. Nice!

## Loading indicator

Firebase is pretty quick to load, but if our users are on slow connections, they will see a blank screen until their messages load, and be wondering, "Where are all my awesome chats?" Let's give them a loading indicator.

Inside our `ChatContainer`, we only want to show the messages if a prop called `messagesLoaded` is true (which we'll define in a moment). We will make the rendering of our message container conditional on that prop. We can do so using a **ternerary** statement.

Ternerary statements in JavaScript are a short way of doing if else. Instead of if (true) { // this code }, else { // that code }, we can write true ? // this code : // that code, which is short and sweet.

The code looks like this:

```
// Beginning of ChatContainer
<Header>
  <button className="red" onClick={this.handleLogout}>
    Logout
  </button>
</Header>
{this.props.messagesLoaded ? (
  <div
    id="message-container"
    ref={element => {
      this.messageContainer = element;
    }}>
    {this.props.messages.map((msg, i) => (
      <div
        key={msg.id}
        className={`message ${this.props.user.email === msg.author &&
          'mine'}`}>
        <p>{msg.msg}</p>
        {this.getAuthor(msg, this.props.messages[i + 1])}
      </div>
    ))}
  </div>
) : (
  <div id="loading-container">
    <img src="/assets/icon.png" alt="logo" id="loader" />
  </div>
)}
<div id="chat-input">
// Rest of ChatContainer
```

Take a moment to read this closely, and ensure that you understand exactly what's going on. Ternerary statements are common in React, simply because they make it easy to conditionally render JSX. If everything is right, you should see the following, with a pulsing animation to the logo:

The next step is to update the `messagesLoaded` prop when the messages load. Let's hop over to `App.js`.

The logic here is simple--when we receive a message value from the Firebase database, if we haven't received a value before (in other words, this is the first message we've received), we know that our messages have loaded for the first time:

```
class App extends Component {
  state = { user: null, messages: [], messagesLoaded: false };

componentDidMount() {
    firebase.auth().onAuthStateChanged(user => {
      if (user) {
        this.setState({ user });
      } else {
        this.props.history.push('/login');
```

```
      }
    });
    firebase
      .database()
      .ref('/messages')
      .on('value', snapshot => {
        this.onMessage(snapshot);
        if (!this.state.messagesLoaded) {
          this.setState({ messagesLoaded: true });
        }
      });
  }

<Route exact path="/" render={() => (
  <ChatContainer
    messagesLoaded={this.state.messagesLoaded}
    onSubmit={this.handleSubmitMessage}
    messages={this.state.messages}
    user={this.state.user} />
)} />
```

Now, if you reload the app page, you should briefly see the loading indicator (depending on your internet connection), and then see the messages displayed.

Here's the code for `ChatContainer` so far:

```
import React, { Component } from 'react';
import { Link } from 'react-router-dom';
import ReactDOM from 'react-dom';
import Header from './Header';

export default class ChatContainer extends Component {
  state = { newMessage: '' };

  componentDidMount() {
    this.scrollToBottom();
  }

  componentDidUpdate(previousProps) {
    if (previousProps.messages.length !== this.props.messages.length) {
      this.scrollToBottom();
    }
  }

  scrollToBottom = () => {
    const messageContainer = ReactDOM.findDOMNode(this.messageContainer);
    if (messageContainer) {
      messageContainer.scrollTop = messageContainer.scrollHeight;
```

```
    }
  };

  handleLogout = () => {
    firebase.auth().signOut();
  };

  handleInputChange = e => {
    this.setState({ newMessage: e.target.value });
  };

  handleSubmit = () => {
    this.props.onSubmit(this.state.newMessage);
    this.setState({ newMessage: '' });
  };

  handleKeyDown = e => {
    if (e.key === 'Enter') {
      e.preventDefault();
      this.handleSubmit();
    }
  };

  getAuthor = (msg, nextMsg) => {
    if (!nextMsg || nextMsg.author !== msg.author) {
      return (
        <p className="author">
          <Link to={`/users/${msg.user_id}`}>{msg.author}</Link>
        </p>
      );
    }
  };

  render() {
    return (
      <div id="ChatContainer" className="inner-container">
        <Header>
          <button className="red" onClick={this.handleLogout}>
            Logout
          </button>
        </Header>
        {this.props.messagesLoaded ? (
          <div
            id="message-container"
            ref={element => {
              this.messageContainer = element;
            }}>
            {this.props.messages.map((msg, i) => (
```

```
        <div
          key={msg.id}
          className={`message ${this.props.user.email ===
                                          msg.author &&
            'mine'}`}>
          <p>{msg.msg}</p>
          {this.getAuthor(msg, this.props.messages[i + 1])}
        </div>
      ))}
    </div>
  ) : (
    <div id="loading-container">
      <img src="/assets/icon.png" alt="logo" id="loader" />
    </div>
  )}
  <div id="chat-input">
    <textarea
      placeholder="Add your message..."
      onChange={this.handleInputChange}
      onKeyDown={this.handleKeyDown}
      value={this.state.newMessage}
    />
    <button onClick={this.handleSubmit}>
      <svg viewBox="0 0 24 24">
        <path fill="#424242"
          d="M2,21L23,12L2,3V10L17,12L2,14V21Z" />
      </svg>
    </button>
  </div>
  </div>
);
  }
}
```

Our app is so close to complete. The last step is the user profile page.

# The Profile page

The code for UserContainer will be the same as ChatContainer, with two major differences:

- We only want to show the messages from our messages array that match the ID from the URL parameters
- We want to show the author email at the top of page, before any other messages

Firstly, in `App.js`, convert the `UserContainer` route to use the `render` prop, the same as `ChatContainer`, and pass in the following props:

```
<Route
  path="/users/:id"
  render={({ history, match }) => (
    <UserContainer
      messages={this.state.messages}
      messagesLoaded={this.state.messagesLoaded}
      userID={match.params.id}
    />
  )}
/>
```

Note that React Router automatically gives us the history and match `props` in our `render` method, which we use here to grab the user ID from the URL parameters.

Then, in `UserContainer`, let's set up our loading indicator. Also, ensure that you give `UserContainer` a `className` of `inner-container` for CSS purposes:

```
<div id="UserContainer" className="inner-container">
  <Header>
    <Link to="/">
      <button className="red">Back To Chat</button>
    </Link>
  </Header>
  {this.props.messagesLoaded ? (
    <h1>Messages go here</h1>
  ) : (
    <div id="loading-container">
      <img src="/assets/icon.png" alt="logo" id="loader" />
    &lt;/div>
  )}
</div>
```

For displaying our messages, we only want to show the ones where `msg.user_id` equals our `props.userID`. Instead of our callback for `Array.map()`, we can just add an `if` statement:

```
{this.props.messagesLoaded ? (
  <div id="message-container">
    {this.props.messages.map(msg => {
      if (msg.user_id === this.props.userID) {
        return (
          <div key={msg.id} className="message">
            <p>{msg.msg}</p>
```

```
            </div>
        );
    }
    })}
    </div>
) : (
    <div id="loading-container">
        <img src="/assets/icon.png" alt="logo" id="loader" />
    </div>
)}
```

This should only show messages from the author whose profile we are on. However, we now need to display the author email at the top.

The challenge is that we won't know the user email until we've loaded the messages, and are iterating over the first message that matches the ID, so we can't use the index of `map()`, like we did before, and we can't use a prop.

Instead, we'll add a `class` property to track whether we've shown the user email already.

Declare it at the top of `UserContainer`:

```
export default class UserContainer extends Component {
    renderedUserEmail = false;

    render() {
        return (
```

Then, we'll call a `getAuthor` method in the code:

```
<div id="message-container">
    {this.props.messages.map(msg => {
        if (msg.user_id === this.props.userID) {
            return (
                <div key={msg.id} className="message">
                    {this.getAuthor(msg.author)}
                    <p>{msg.msg}</p>
                </div>
            );
        }
    })}
</div>
```

This checks to see if we've rendered the author already, and if not, returns it:

```
getAuthor = author => {
  if (!this.renderedUserEmail) {
    this.renderedUserEmail = true;
    return <p className="author">{author}</p>;
  }
};
```

A little bit of a roundabout route--for our production application, we'd probably want to add more sophisticated logic to only load the messages from that author. However, this will do just fine for our prototype.

Here's the full code for `UserContainer`:

```
import React, { Component } from 'react';
import { Link } from 'react-router-dom';
import Header from './Header';

export default class UserContainer extends Component {
  renderedUserEmail = false;

  getAuthor = author => {
    if (!this.renderedUserEmail) {
      this.renderedUserEmail = true;
      return <p className="author">{author}</p>;
    }
  };

  render() {
    return (
      <div id="UserContainer" className="inner-container">
        <Header>
          <Link to="/">
            <button className="red">Back To Chat</button>
          </Link>
        </Header>
        {this.props.messagesLoaded ? (
          <div id="message-container">
            {this.props.messages.map(msg => {
              if (msg.user_id === this.props.userID) {
                return (
                  <div key={msg.id} className="message">
                    {this.getAuthor(msg.author)}
                    <p>{msg.msg}</p>
                  </div>
                );
              }
```

```
            })}
          </div>
      ) : (
          <div id="loading-container">
            <img src="/assets/icon.png" alt="logo" id="loader" />
          </div>
      )}
      </div>
    );
  }
}
```

# Summary

That's it! We've built our complete React application. Your friend is thrilled with the final product, but we're far from done.

We've built a web application. It looks pretty good, but it is not yet a progressive web app. There's a lot more work to be done, but this is where the fun starts.

Our next step is to start converting this app into a PWA. We'll start with looking at how we can make our web app more like a native app, and dive into one of the most exciting pieces of web technology of recent years--service workers.

# 7
# Adding a Service Worker

Welcome to our first big step into the world of Progressive Web Applications. This chapter will be devoted to creating our first service worker which, in turn, will unlock much of the functionality that makes PWAs so special.

We've talked previously about PWAs bridging web apps and native applications. The way they do this is through service workers. Service workers make things such as push notifications and offline access possible. They're an exciting new technology with many applications (more and more emerging each year); if one piece of tech will transform web development in the next five years, it's service workers.

However, enough hype; let's dive in to what exactly a service worker is.

In this chapter, we'll cover the following topics:

- What is a service worker?
- The service worker life cycle
- How to register a service worker on our page

## What is a service worker?

A **service worker** is a bit of JavaScript that sits between our application and the network.

You can think of a script that runs outside the context of our application, but with which we can communicate from within the bounds of our code. It's a piece of our application, but separate from the rest.

The easiest example is in the context of caching files (which we'll explore in the upcoming chapters). Let's say that our application, when the user navigates to `https://chatastrophe.com`, goes and fetches our `icon.png` file.

A service worker, if we configure it, will sit between our app and the network. When our app requests the icon file, the service worker intercepts that request and checks the local cache for the file. If found, it returns it; no network request is made. Only if it doesn't find the file in the cache does it let the network request go through; after the download is complete, it puts the file in the cache.

You can see where the term "worker" comes from--our service worker is a busy little bee.

Let's look at another example; push notifications (sneak preview of `Chapter 9`, *Making Our App Installable with a Manifest*). Most push notifications work this way--when a certain event happens (a user sends a new chat message), a messaging service is alerted (in our case, the message service is managed by Firebase). The messaging service sends an alert to the relevant registered users (who are registered via their devices), and then their devices create the notification (ding!).

The problem with this flow, in a web app context, is that our application stops running when the user is not on the page, so we won't be able to notify them unless their app is already open, which completely defeats the point of push notifications.

Service workers solve this problem by always being "on" and listening for messages. Now, the messaging service can alert our service worker, which displays a message to the user. Our application code is never actually involved, so it doesn't matter whether it's running or not.

This is exciting stuff, but with any new technology, there's a few rough edges, and some things to watch out for.

# The service worker life cycle

The life of your service worker begins when a user first visits your page. The service worker is downloaded and begins running. It may go idle for a time when not needed, but can then restart when required.

This **always on** functionality is what makes the service workers useful for push notifications. It also makes service workers a bit unintuitive to work with (more on that to come). However, let's take a deep look at the life and death of a service worker on a typical page.

First, the service worker is installed, if possible. All service worker installations will start with a check to see whether the technology is supported by the user's browser. As of now, Firefox, Chrome, and Opera have full support, and other browsers do not. Apple, for one, views service workers as **experimental technology**, indicating that they're still on the fence about the whole thing.

If the user's browser is modern enough, the installation begins. The script (for example, `sw.js`) is installed (or rather, registered) within a certain scope. **Scope**, in this case, refers to what paths of the website it is concerned with. A global scope will take `'/'`, for example, all paths on the site, but you can also limit your service worker to `'/users'`; for example, to only cache certain parts of the application. We'll discuss more about scope in the caching chapters.

Once registered, the service worker is activated. The activation event also occurs whenever the service worker is required, for example, when a push notification comes in. The activation and deactivation of service workers means that you cannot persist state within a service worker; it's just a bit of code ran in reaction to events, rather than a full-blown application of its own. That's an important distinction to remember, lest we ask too much of our workers.

The service worker will be idle until an event occurs. As of now, there are two events that service workers react to: a `fetch` event (also known as a network request from the application) and a `message` (also known as an interaction from either the application code or a messaging service). We can register listeners for these events within the service worker, and then react as appropriate.

The service worker code will update under two conditions: 24 hours has elapsed (in which case it stops and redownloads a method to prevent broken code from causing too much annoyance), or the user visits the page and the `sw.js` file has changed. Every time the user visits the app, the service worker compares its current code with the `sw.js` served by the site, and if there is even a byte of difference, the new `sw.js` is downloaded and registered.

That's the basic technical overview of service workers and how they work. It may seem complicated, but the good news is that using service workers is relatively straightforward; you can get a simple one up and running in a matter of minutes, which is exactly what we'll do next!

# Registering our first service worker

Remember the distinction about service workers--they are a piece of our site, but run outside our application code. With that in mind, our service worker will live inside `public/` folder, and not in `src/` folder.

Then, create a file called `sw.js` in your `public/` folder. We'll keep it simple for now; just add a single `console.log` inside:

```
console.log("Service worker running!");
```

The real work (registering the service worker) will be done inside our `index.html`. For this process, we want to do the following:

1. Check whether the browser supports service workers.
2. Wait for the page to load.
3. Register the service worker.
4. Log out the result.

Let's move through the steps one by one. First, let's create an empty `script` tag below our Firebase initialization, inside `public/index.html`:

```
<body>
  <div id="root"></div>
  <script src="/secrets.js"></script>
  <script
src="https://www.gstatic.com/firebasejs/4.1.2/firebase.js"></script>
  <script>
    // Initialize Firebase
    var config = {
      apiKey: window.apiKey,
      authDomain: "chatastrophe-77bac.firebaseapp.com",
      databaseURL: "https://chatastrophe-77bac.firebaseio.com",
      projectId: "chatastrophe-77bac",
      storageBucket: "chatastrophe-77bac.appspot.com",
      messagingSenderId: "85734589405"
    };
    window.firebase = firebase;
    firebase.initializeApp(config);
  </script>
  <script>
    // Service worker code here.
  </script>
```

# Checking for browser support

Checking whether the user's browser can handle service workers is very easy. In our script tag, we'll add a simple `if` statement:

```
<script>
  if ('serviceWorker' in navigator) {
    // register
  } else {
    console.log('service worker is not supported');
  }
</script>
```

Here, we check the `window.navigator` object for any service worker support. The navigator can also be used (via its `userAgent` property) to check what browser the user has, though we won't need that here.

# Listening for the page load

We don't want to register our service worker until the page has finished loading; there's no point, and it can lead to complications, so we'll add an event listener to the window for the `'load'` event:

```
<script>
  if ('serviceWorker' in navigator) {
    window.addEventListener('load', function() {

    });
  } else {
    console.log('service worker is not supported');
  }
</script>
```

# Registering the service worker

As we noted earlier, the `window.navigator` has a `serviceWorker` property, the existence of which confirms browser support for service workers. We can also use that same object to register our service worker, via its `register` function. I know, it's shocking stuff.

We call `navigator.serviceWorker.register`, and pass in the path to our service worker file:

```
<script>
 if ('serviceWorker' in navigator) {
   window.addEventListener('load', function() {
     navigator.serviceWorker.register('sw.js')
   });
 } else {
   console.log('service worker is not supported');
 }
</script>
```

# Logging out the result

Lastly, let's add some `console.log`s so that we know the result of the registration. Luckily, `navigator.serviceWorker.register` returns a promise:

```
<script>
  if ('serviceWorker' in navigator) {
    window.addEventListener('load', function() {
      navigator.serviceWorker.register('sw.js').then(function(registration)
{
        // Registration was successful
        console.log('Registered!');
      }, function(err) {
        // registration failed :(
        console.log('ServiceWorker registration failed: ', err);
      }).catch(function(err) {
        console.log(err);
      });
    });
  } else {
    console.log('service worker is not supported');
  }
</script>
```

Okay, let's test this all out! Reload the page, and if all is good, you should see the following in your console:

```
Service worker running!                      sw.js:1
Registered!                                  (index):39
>
```

You can also check it by navigating to the **Application** tab in DevTools, and then to the **Service Workers** tab:

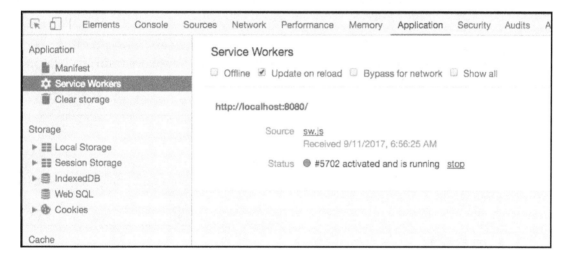

I would recommend taking the opportunity to check the **Update on reload** button at this time. This ensures that your service worker is refreshed every time you refresh the page (remember the normal service worker life cycle we discussed earlier). Why take this precaution? We're stepping into the world of cached code, where the browser may think your service worker hasn't changed, when it actually has. This checkbox just ensures that you're always dealing with the freshest build of sw.js.

Okay, we've registered a worker! Fantastic. Let's take a moment to go through the service worker life cycle from within our sw.js.

# Experiencing the service worker life cycle

The first event that a service worker experiences is the `'install'` event. This is when a user first starts up a PWA. The standard user will only experience this once.

To tap into this event, all we have to do is add an event listener to our service worker itself. To do that from within `sw.js`, we use the `self` keyword:

```
self.addEventListener('install', function() {
  console.log('Install!');
});
```

When you reload the page, you should see `'Install!'` appear in the console. In fact, you should see it every time you reload the page, unless you uncheck the **Update on reload** option under **Application | Service Workers**. Then, you will only see it the first time.

Next up is the `activate` event. This event is triggered when the service worker first registers, before the registration completes. In other words, it should occur under the same situations as install, only later:

```
self.addEventListener('activate', function() {
    console.log('Activate!');
});
```

The last event we want to cover is the `'fetch'` event. This event is called whenever the application makes a network request. It's called with an event object that has a request URL, which we can log out:

```
self.addEventListener('fetch', function(event) {
    console.log('Fetch!', event.request);
});
```

After adding this in, we should see a very cluttered console:

```
Fetch!                                        firebase-messaging-sw.js:11
▶ Request {method: "GET", url: "http://localhost:8080/secrets.js", headers: Header
  "http://localhost:8080/", referrerPolicy: "no-referrer-when-downgrade", …}
Fetch!                                        firebase-messaging-sw.js:11
▶ Request {method: "GET", url: "https://www.gstatic.com/firebasejs/4.3.0/firebase.
  "http://localhost:8080/", referrerPolicy: "no-referrer-when-downgrade", …}
Fetch!                                        firebase-messaging-sw.js:11
▶ Request {method: "GET", url: "http://localhost:8080/bundle.js", headers: Headers
  "http://localhost:8080/", referrerPolicy: "no-referrer-when-downgrade", …}
Fetch!                                        firebase-messaging-sw.js:11
▶ Request {method: "POST", url: "https://securetoken.googleapis.com/v1/token?key=A
  headers: Headers, referrer: "http://localhost:8080/", referrerPolicy: "no-referr
[HMR] Waiting for update signal from WDS...          bundle.js:6543
[HMR] Waiting for update signal from WDS...          bundle.js:6543
Fetch!                                        firebase-messaging-sw.js:11
▶ Request {method: "GET", url: "http://localhost:8080/assets/icon.png", headers: H
  "http://localhost:8080/", referrerPolicy: "no-referrer-when-downgrade", …}
Registered!                                          (index):35
Fetch!                                        firebase-messaging-sw.js:11
  Request {method: "GET", url: "http://localhost:8080/sockjs-node/info?
▶ t=1506464637957", headers: Headers, referrer: "http://localhost:8080/", referrer
  referrer-when-downgrade", …}
```

You can delete all the `console.log`s in the service worker for now, but we will use each of these event listeners in the future.

Next, we'll look at hooking into the Firebase messaging service, to lay the groundwork for push notifications.

# Adding Firebase to our service worker

Our goal for the rest of the chapter is to integrate Firebase into our service worker so that it is ready to receive push notifications and display them.

This is a big project. We won't be able to actually display push notifications until the end of the next chapter. However, here we'll see how to integrate third-party services into service workers, and dive a little more into the theory behind service workers.

# Naming our service worker

The service we will use to send push notifications to user devices is called **Firebase Cloud Messaging**, or **FCM**. FCM works on the web by looking for a service worker and then sending it a message (containing the notification details). The service worker then displays the notification.

By default, FCM looks for a service worker named `firebase-messaging-sw.js`. You can change that using `firebase.messaging().useServiceWorker` and passing a service worker registration object. For our purposes, however, it will be more straightforward to simply rename our service worker. Let's do so; change the filename in `public/` and in the registration in `index.html`:

```
<script>
  if ('serviceWorker' in navigator) {
    window.addEventListener('load', function() {
      navigator.serviceWorker.register('firebase-messaging-
sw.js').then(function(registration) {
        // Registration was successful
        console.log('Registered!');
      }, function(err) {
        // registration failed :(
        console.log('ServiceWorker registration failed: ', err);
      }).catch(function(err) {
        console.log(err);
      });
    });
  } else {
    console.log('service worker is not supported');
  }
</script>
```

Once that's done, we can start initializing Firebase inside our service worker.

Let's say it again; a service worker is not linked to your application code. This means that it does not have access to our current Firebase initialization. We can reinitialize Firebase inside our service worker, though, and only keep what's relevant--the `messagingSenderId`. You can get your `messagingSenderId` from the Firebase console or your `secrets.js` file.

 If you're concerned about security, ensure that you add `public/firebase-messaging-sw.js` to your `.gitignore`, though keeping your `messagingSenderId` private is not as important as keeping your API key secret.

```
// firebase-messaging-sw.js
firebase.initializeApp({
  'messagingSenderId': '85734589405'
});
```

We also need to import the parts of Firebase we need at the top of the file, which include the app library and the `messaging` library:

```
importScripts('https://www.gstatic.com/firebasejs/3.9.0/firebase-app.js');
importScripts('https://www.gstatic.com/firebasejs/3.9.0/firebase-messaging.
js');
```

Once that's done, we should be able to `console.log` out `firebase.messaging();`:

```
importScripts('https://www.gstatic.com/firebasejs/3.9.0/firebase-app.js');
importScripts('https://www.gstatic.com/firebasejs/3.9.0/firebase-messaging.
js');

firebase.initializeApp({
    'messagingSenderId': '85734589405'
});

console.log(firebase.messaging());
```

You should see the following:

```
▼ P {a: e, l: "85734589405", c: B, app: e, INTERNAL: {…}, …}
  ▶ INTERNAL: {delete: f}
  ▶ a: e {service: "messaging", serviceName: "Messaging", errors: {…}, pattern: /\{\$([^}]+)}/g}
  ▶ app: e {firebase_: {…}, isDeleted_: false, services_: {…}, name_: "[DEFAULT]", options_: {…}, …}
    b: null
  ▶ c: B {a: null}
    l: "85734589405"
  ▶ __proto__: I
```

This means our Firebase is up and running inside our service worker!

> If you're still seeing the logs from our old `sw.js`, go to the **Application |
> Service Workers** tab of DevTools and **Unregister** it. This is a good
> example of how service workers will persist even if they're not being
> reregistered.

As explained earlier, a service worker is an always-running piece of code (though not perfectly accurate--think of the life cycle of such workers--which is a good way to think of them). This means it will always be waiting for FCM to tell it that there's a message coming in.

However, right now, we don't have any messages coming. The next step is to start configuring when push notifications get sent, and how to display them!

# Summary

In this chapter, we learned the basics of service workers, and got one up and running. Our next step is to start using it. Specifically, we want to use it to listen for notifications, and then display them to the user. Let's take another big step towards making our PWA feel like a native app by setting up push notifications.

# 8
# Using a Service Worker to Send Push Notifications

In this chapter, we will complete our application's process for sending push notifications. The implementation is a little complicated; it requires many moving pieces to get things working (in my experience, this is true of any push notifications implementation, on mobile or web). The exciting part is that we get to interact with a lot of new areas of knowledge, such as **Device tokens** and **Cloud functions**.

Before we begin, let's take a minute to outline the process for setting up push notifications. As of now, we have our messaging service worker up and running. This service worker will sit there and wait to be called with a new notification. Once that happens, it'll handle everything to do with displaying that notification, so we don't have to worry about that (at least).

What is up to us is sending that message to the service worker. Let's say that we have 1,000 users for our application, each with one unique device. Each device has a unique token, which identifies it to Firebase. We need to keep track of all of those tokens, because when we want to send a notification, we need to tell Firebase exactly what devices to send it to.

So, that's step one--set up and maintain a database table of all tokens for devices using our app. As we'll see, that also necessarily involves asking the user whether they want notifications in the first place.

Once we have our tokens saved, we can then tell Firebase to listen for a new message in the database, and then send a notification to all devices (based on the tokens) with the message details. As a small additional complication, we have to ensure that we don't send the notification to the user who created the message.

This stage (telling Firebase to send a notification) actually takes place outside of our application. It takes place in the mythical "Cloud", where we'll host a function to take care of this process; more on that later.

Our approach to this rather involved piece of engineering will be to approach it slowly, one piece at a time. Ensure that you follow the code examples carefully; the nature of notifications means we won't be able to fully test our implementation until it is complete, so do your best to avoid small errors along the way.

In this chapter, we'll cover these topics:

- Requesting permission to show notifications
- Tracking and saving user tokens
- Using Cloud Functions to send notifications

Alright, let's do it!

# Requesting permission

As the preceding introduction explains, we have a lot of functionality to create in this chapter. In order to keep it all in one place, without cluttering up our `App.js`, we will create a separate JavaScript class to manage everything to do with notifications. This is a pattern I really like with React, to extract functionality not attached to any one component. In our `src/` folder, next to our `components` folder, let's create a folder called `resources`, and within that, a file called `NotificationResource.js`.

The basic outline of our class looks like this:

```
export default class NotificationResource {

}
```

We create a JavaScript class and export it.

> For those unfamiliar with JavaScript classes (especially for those familiar with classes in other languages), I encourage you to read the MDN article explaining the basics, at `https://developer.mozilla.org/en-US/docs/Web/JavaScript/Reference/Classes`.

Let's import it in our `App.js` before we forget:

```
import NotificationResource from '../resources/NotificationResource';
```

When our app starts up, we want to ask the user for permission to send them notifications. Note that Firebase remembers whether the user has already accepted or denied our request, so we won't be bothering them with a popup every time, only if they haven't been asked before.

Here's how we'll approach this process:

1. When our app mounts, we'll create a new instance of the `NotificationResource` class, passing it the Firebase messaging library (we pass this in to save us from having to import it into the `NotificationResource.js` file, since we already have access to it in `App.js`).
2. When the `NotificationResource` class is first instantiated, we'll immediately ask the user for permission, using the Firebase messaging library passed in.

If these steps are clear to you, I encourage you to try implementing them on your own first. If you're totally confused about how we will do this, don't worry, we'll go through it all.

Okay, let's start with our App's `componentDidMount`. This is where we want to create the instance of our `NotificationResource`:

```
componentDidMount() {
    this.notifications = new NotificationResource();
```

We're setting the `NotificationResource` instance to be a property of `App`; this will allow us to access it elsewhere within `App.js`.

As we said earlier, we also want to pass in the Firebase messaging library:

```
componentDidMount() {
    this.notifications = new NotificationResource(firebase.messaging());
```

Every JavaScript class automatically has a `constructor` method that is called when an instance is created. That is what we're called when we say new `NotificationResource()`. Whatever we put inside those brackets is passed as an argument to the constructor.

Let's jump back over to `NotificationResource.js` and set that up:

```
export default class NotificationResource {
  constructor(messaging) {
    console.log("Instantiated!");
  }
}
```

If you start up your app, you should see "Instantiated!" in the console as soon as App mounts.

The next step is to use our messaging library to access the user for permission to send them notifications:

```
export default class NotificationResource {
    constructor(messaging) {
      this.messaging = messaging;
      try {
        this.messaging
          .requestPermission()
          .then(res => {
            console.log('Permission granted');
          })
          .catch(err => {
          console.log('no access', err);
          });
      } catch(err) {
        console.log('No notification support.', err);
      }
  } }
```

We do the same thing we did with the NotificationResource in App with the messaging library, that is, save it as a property of our resource so that we can use it elsewhere. Then, we tap into the requestPermission function.

If we go back to our app, we see this:

Click on **Allow**, and you should see **Permission granted** in the console.

If you've previously built a personal project using localhost:8080 and allowed notifications, you won't see this popup. You can forget your previous preference by clicking on the icon to the left of the URL in the preceding screenshot, and resetting notifications to **Ask**.

Now that we have permission to start bugging our users, we will start keeping track of all their devices, via tokens.

# Tracking tokens

A **token** is a unique identifier for your user's device. It helps Firebase figure out where to send push notifications. In order for our notifications to be sent properly, we need to keep a record of all current device tokens in our database, and ensure that it's up to date.

We can access the token of our user's device via the Firebase `messaging` library. Two methods in particular will be useful: `onTokenRefresh` and `getToken`. Both have fairly self-explanatory names, so we'll dive right into the implementation:

```
export default class NotificationResource {
    constructor(messaging) {
      this.messaging = messaging;
      try {
        this.messaging
          .requestPermission()
          .then(res => {
            console.log('Permission granted');
          })
          .catch(err => {
            console.log('no access', err);
          });
      } catch(err) {
        console.log('No notification support.', err);
      }
  };
    this.messaging.getToken().then(res => {
      console.log(res);
    });
  }
```

You'll see a very long string of numbers and letters when your app refreshes. This is your device's identity. We need to save this to the database.

Whenever the token changes `firebase.messaging().onTokenRefresh` is called. The token can be deleted by our application, or when the user clears browser data, in which case a new one will be generated. When that happens, we'll need to overwrite the old token in our database. The key part is overwriting; if we don't delete the old token, we'll end up wasting Firebase's time by sending to devices that don't exist.

So, we have four steps to cover:

1. When the token changes, get the new token.
2. Look for an existing token in the database.
3. If an old one exists, replace it.
4. Otherwise, add the new token to the database.

There's a bunch of intermediary tasks we'll have to complete in order to finish this checklist, but let's just dive in with this rough plan.

We will add four functions to our `NotificationResource`: `setupTokenRefresh`, `saveTokenToServer`, `findExistingToken`, and `registerToken`. You can see how the last two accord with the last two steps in our checklist.

Let's start with `setupTokenRefresh`. We will call this from our constructor, because it will be in charge of registering the listener for token changes:

```
export default class NotificationResource {
  constructor(messaging) {
    this.messaging = messaging;
    try {
      this.messaging
        .requestPermission()
        .then(res => {
          console.log('Permission granted');
        })
        .catch(err => {
          console.log('no access', err);
        });
    } catch(err) {
      console.log('No notification support.', err);
    }
  }
}
```

This pattern should be familiar after all the "on" listeners we've configured with Firebase.

Next, we'll create `saveTokenToServer`, and call it from `setupTokenRefresh`:

```
setupTokenRefresh() {
  this.messaging.onTokenRefresh(() => {
    this.saveTokenToServer();
  });
}

saveTokenToServer() {
```

```
    // Get token
    // Look for existing token
    // If it exists, replace
    // Otherwise, create a new one
}
```

Okay, now we can move through those comments one by one. We already know how to get the token:

```
saveTokenToServer() {
    this.messaging.getToken().then(res => {
        // Look for existing token
        // If it exists, replace
        // Otherwise, create a new one
    });
}
```

For the next step, look for the existing token; we don't currently have access to the previous tokens saved in our database (okay, there aren't any yet, but there will be).

So, we need to create a table in our database to save our tokens. We'll call it `fcmTokens` for ease. It doesn't exist yet, but it will as soon as we send some data to it. That's the beauty of the Firebase data--you can send data to a non-existent table, and it will be created and populated.

Just as we did for messages in `App.js`, let's add a listener for values from the `/fcmTokens` table inside the constructor of `NotificationResource`:

```
export default class NotificationResource {
    allTokens = [];
    tokensLoaded = false;

    constructor(messaging, database) {
        this.database = database;
        this.messaging = messaging;
            try {
            this.messaging
                .requestPermission()
                .then(res => {
                    console.log('Permission granted');
                })
                .catch(err => {
                    console.log('no access', err);
                });
            } catch(err) {
            console.log('No notification support.', err);
        }};
```

```
      this.setupTokenRefresh();
      this.database.ref('/fcmTokens').on('value', snapshot => {
        this.allTokens = snapshot.val();
        this.tokensLoaded = true;
      });
    }
```

You'll note that we now expect a database instance to be passed into the constructor. Let's hop back over to App.js to set that up:

```
componentDidMount() {
    this.notifications = new NotificationResource(
        firebase.messaging(),
        firebase.database()
    );
```

Okay, this is perfect.

If you console.log out snapshot.val() inside of the database listener, it'll be null, since there are no values in our /fcmTokens table. Let's work on registering one:

```
saveTokenToServer() {
    this.messaging.getToken().then(res => {
      if (this.tokensLoaded) {
        const existingToken = this.findExistingToken(res);
        if (existingToken) {
          // Replace existing toke
        } else {
          // Create a new one
        }
      }
    });
  }
```

If the tokens are loaded, we can check for an existing one. If the tokens are not loaded, do nothing. This may seem odd, but we want to ensure that we don't create duplicate values.

How do we find an existing token? Well, in our constructor, we saved the result of loading the token values in the database to this.allTokens. We will simply loop through them and see whether any of them match the res variable generated from getToken:

```
findExistingToken(tokenToSave) {
    for (let tokenKey in this.allTokens) {
      const token = this.allTokens[tokenKey].token;
      if (token === tokenToSave) {
        return tokenKey;
      }
    }
```

```
    }
    return false;
}
```

The important part of this method is that `tokenToSave` will be a string (the random assortment of numbers and letters seen earlier), and `this.allTokens` will be a collection of token objects loaded from the database and hence the `this.allTokens[tokenObject].token` business.

`findExistingToken` will thus either return the key of the token object that matches, or false. From there, we can either update that existing token object, or create a new one. We'll see why it's important to return the key (rather than the object itself) when we try to update the token.

# Attaching a user to the token

Before we move on to covering the two cases though, let's take a step back and think about how our push notifications will work, because there's an important caveat we need to cover.

When a user sends a message, we want to notify every user, except the user who created the message (that will be infuriating), so we need some way to send a notification to every token in our database, except for the ones that belong to the user who sent the message.

How will we be able to prevent that? How can we match a user's message with a user's token?

Well, we have access to the user ID in the message object (that is, we always save the ID along with the message content). What if we did something similar with the token, and saved the user ID along with it, so we can be sure to identify which user belongs to which device?

This seems like a pretty simple solution, but that means we need access to the current user's ID inside `NotificationResource`. Let's do that right away, and then get back to writing and updating tokens.

# Changing the user inside NotificationResource

We already have a method to handle user changes inside App.js--our old friend, onAuthStateChanged. Let's hook in to that, and use that to call a method inside NotificationResource:

```
componentDidMount() {
    this.notifications = new NotificationResource(firebase.messaging(),
  firebase.database());
    firebase.auth().onAuthStateChanged((user) => {
        if (user) {
          this.setState({ user });
          this.listenForMessages();
          this.notifications.changeUser(user);
        } else {
          this.props.history.push('/login')
        }
    });
```

Then, inside NotificationResource:

```
changeUser(user) {
    this.user = user;
  }
```

Incidentally, this helps us solve another problem with tokens. As noted earlier, onTokenRefresh is called when a new token is generated, either because the user deleted browser data or because the web app deleted the previous token. However, if we're saving the user ID along with the token, we need to ensure that we update that ID when the user changes, so we'll have to call our saveTokenToServer method every time the user changes:

```
changeUser(user) {
    this.user = user;
    this.saveTokenToServer();
  }
```

Okay, now we can go back to our if-else statement inside saveTokenToServer, and start saving some tokens.

# Creating a new token

Let's start with covering the latter case, creating a new token. We'll make a new method called `registerToken`, passing in the result of the `getToken` call:

```
saveTokenToServer() {
    this.messaging.getToken().then(res => {
      if (this.tokensLoaded) {
        const existingToken = this.findExistingToken(res);
        if (existingToken) {
          // Replace existing token
        } else {
          this.registerToken(res);
        }
      }
    });
}
```

Then, our new method:

```
registerToken(token) {
    firebase
      .database()
      .ref('fcmTokens/')
      .push({
        token: token,
        user_id: this.user.uid
      });
}
```

We save the token, along with the user ID. Perfect.

# Updating an existing token

We'll do something similar with updating a token, but this time we need to access the existing token in the database.

Add a `console.log` here for testing purposes:

```
saveTokenToServer() {
    this.messaging.getToken().then(res => {
      if (this.tokensLoaded) {
        const existingToken = this.findExistingToken(res);
        if (existingToken) {
          console.log(existingToken);
        } else {
```

```
            this.registerToken(res);
        }
      }
    });
  }
```

Then, try logging in and out of the app with different users. You should see the same `existingToken` key each time:

We can use this to grab the existing entry from the `fcmToken` table in our database, and update it:

```
saveTokenToServer() {
  this.messaging.getToken().then(res => {
    if (this.tokensLoaded) {
      const existingToken = this.findExistingToken(res);
      if (existingToken) {
        firebase
          .database()
          .ref(`/fcmTokens/${existingToken}`)
          .set({
            token: res,
            user_id: this.user.uid
          });
      } else {
        this.registerToken(res);
      }
    }
  });
}
```

Okay, that was a lot. Let's double-check that this is working correctly. Go to `console.firebase.com` and check the **Database** tab. Try logging in and out of the app again with two different users. You should see the matching token entry update its user ID each time. Then, try logging in on a different device (after doing another firebase deploy) and see another token appear. Magic!

We now have a table of tokens for every device that uses our app, along with the ID of the user last associated with that device. We're now ready to move to the best part of push notifications--actually sending them.

Here's the final `NotificationResource.js`:

```
export default class NotificationResource {
  allTokens = [];
  tokensLoaded = false;
  user = null;

  constructor(messaging, database) {
    this.messaging = messaging;
    this.database = database;
        try {
      this.messaging
        .requestPermission()
        .then(res => {
          console.log('Permission granted');
        })
        .catch(err => {
          console.log('no access', err);
        });
      } catch(err) {
        console.log('No notification support.', err);
      };
    this.setupTokenRefresh();
    this.database.ref('/fcmTokens').on('value', snapshot => {
      this.allTokens = snapshot.val();
      this.tokensLoaded = true;
    });
  }

  setupTokenRefresh() {
    this.messaging.onTokenRefresh(() => {
      this.saveTokenToServer();
    });
  }

  saveTokenToServer() {
    this.messaging.getToken().then(res => {
```

```
      if (this.tokensLoaded) {
        const existingToken = this.findExistingToken(res);
        if (existingToken) {
          firebase
            .database()
            .ref(`/fcmTokens/${existingToken}`)
            .set({
              token: res,
              user_id: this.user.uid
            });
        } else {
          this.registerToken(res);
        }
      }
    });
  }

  registerToken(token) {
    firebase
      .database()
      .ref('fcmTokens/')
      .push({
        token: token,
        user_id: this.user.uid
      });
  }

  findExistingToken(tokenToSave) {
    for (let tokenKey in this.allTokens) {
      const token = this.allTokens[tokenKey].token;
      if (token === tokenToSave) {
        return tokenKey;
      }
    }
    return false;
  }

  changeUser(user) {
    this.user = user;
    this.saveTokenToServer();
  }
}
```

# Sending push notifications

Way back at the beginning of this book, when we initialized Firebase, we checked an option for **Functions**. This created a folder in our root directory called `functions`, which we have ignored as of yet (if you don't have this folder, you can run `firebase init` again, and ensure that you check off both **Functions** and **Hosting** for the first question. Reference the chapter on Firebase for more).

The `functions` folder allows us to use Firebase Cloud Functions. Here's how Google defines them:

> *"Cloud Functions gives developers access to Firebase and Google Cloud events, along with scalable computing power to run code in response to those events."*

That's the simplest definition--code that runs in response to events, outside of our application. We extract a bit of functionality that doesn't belong to any particular instance of our app (because it concerns all instances of our app) to the Cloud, and have it run automatically by Firebase.

Let's open up `functions /index.js` and get to work.

# Writing our Cloud function

First, we can initialize our app, as follows:

```
const functions = require('firebase-functions');
const admin = require('firebase-admin');
admin.initializeApp(functions.config().firebase);
```

Cloud functions = code run in response to events, so what's our event?

We want to notify the user when a new message is created. So, the event is a new message, or, more specifically, when a new entry is created in the messages table of our database.

We'll define the export of our `index.js` to be a function called `sendNotifications`, which defines a listener for the `onWrite` event of `/messages`:

```
exports.sendNotifications = functions.database
  .ref('/messages/{messageId}')
  .onWrite(event => {});
```

Everything else in this section will take place in the event listener.

First, we grab the snapshot from the event:

```
const snapshot = event.data;
```

Right now, we don't support editing messages; but one day we might. We don't want a push notification in that event, so we'll return early if onWrite is triggered by an update (the snapshot has a previous value):

```
const snapshot = event.data;
if (snapshot.previous.val()) {
   return;
}
```

Then, we'll construct our notification. We define an object with a nested notification object, with a title, body, icon, and click_action:

```
const payload = {
   notification: {
      title: `${snapshot.val().author}`,
      body: `${snapshot.val().msg}`,
      icon: 'assets/icon.png',
      click_action: `https://${functions.config().firebase.authDomain}`
   }
};
```

The title comes from the user email associated with the message. The body is the message itself. Both of those are wrapped in template strings to ensure that they come out as strings. It's just a safety thing!

Then, we use our app icon as the icon for the notification. Note the path--the icon doesn't actually exist in our functions folder, but since it will be deployed to the root of our app (it's in the build folder), we can reference it.

Lastly, our click_action should take our user to the app. We grab the domain URL via our config.

The next step is to send payload to the relevant devices. Buckle up, this will be a good chunk of code.

# Sending to the tokens

Let's write out the steps we need to take:

1. Get a list of all tokens in our database.
2. Filter that list for only the tokens that don't belong to the user who sent the message.
3. Send the notification to the devices.
4. If any devices fail to receive the notification due to an invalid or unregistered token, remove their tokens from the database.

The last step is to keep things clean by periodically removing invalid tokens from our database.

Okay, sounds like fun. Remember that this is all within the event listener of `onWrite`. Here's the first step:

```
return admin
    .database()
    .ref('fcmTokens')
    .once('value')
    .then(allTokens => {
      if (allTokens.val()) {
      }
    });
```

This uses the database `.once` method to grab a one-time look at the token table. From there, we can proceed if we actually have some tokens saved.

To filter our results, we'll do a loop very similar to our `findExistingToken` method:

```
    .then(allTokens => {
      if (allTokens.val()) {
        const tokens = [];
        for (let fcmTokenKey in allTokens.val()) {
          const fcmToken = allTokens.val()[fcmTokenKey];
          if (fcmToken.user_id !== snapshot.val().user_id) {
            tokens.push(fcmToken.token);
          }
        }
      }
    });
```

We loop through all tokens, and if the `user_id` does not match the `user_id` of the message, we push it into our array of valid tokens.

Time for the third step; send the notification to every device, as illustrated:

```
.then(allTokens => {
  if (allTokens.val()) {
    const tokens = [];
    for (let fcmTokenKey in allTokens.val()) {
      const fcmToken = allTokens.val()[fcmTokenKey];
      if (fcmToken.user_id !== snapshot.val().user_id) {
        tokens.push(fcmToken.token);
      }
    }
    if (tokens.length > 0) {
      return admin
        .messaging()
        .sendToDevice(tokens, payload)
        .then(response => {});
    }
  }
});
```

This is pretty straightforward. We pass `sendToDevice` an array of tokens, and our payload object.

Lastly, let's do the cleanup:

```
if (tokens.length > 0) {
  return admin
    .messaging()
    .sendToDevice(tokens, payload)
    .then(response => {
      const tokensToRemove = [];
      response.results.forEach((result, index) => {
        const error = result.error;
        if (error) {
          console.error(
            'Failure sending notification to',
            tokens[index],
            error
          );
          if (
            error.code === 'messaging/invalid-registration-token' ||
            error.code ===
              'messaging/registration-token-not-registered'
          ) {
            tokensToRemove.push(
              allTokens.ref.child(tokens[index]).remove()
            );
          }
        }
```

```
    }
  });
  return Promise.all(tokensToRemove);
});
}
```

This code should be simple to look through, except perhaps returning the `Promise.all`. The reason for that is that called `remove()` on each token entry returns a promise, and we simply return the resolution of all such promises.

Here's the final file:

```
const functions = require('firebase-functions');
const admin = require('firebase-admin');
admin.initializeApp(functions.config().firebase);

exports.sendNotifications = functions.database
  .ref('/messages/{messageId}')
  .onWrite(event => {
    const snapshot = event.data;
    if (snapshot.previous.val()) {
      return;
    }
    const payload = {
      notification: {
        title: `${snapshot.val().author}`,
        body: `${snapshot.val().msg}`,
        icon: 'assets/icon.png',
        click_action: `https://${functions.config().firebase.authDomain}`
      }
    };
    return admin
      .database()
      .ref('fcmTokens')
      .once('value')
      .then(allTokens => {
        if (allTokens.val()) {
          const tokens = [];
          for (let fcmTokenKey in allTokens.val()) {
            const fcmToken = allTokens.val()[fcmTokenKey];
            if (fcmToken.user_id !== snapshot.val().user_id) {
              tokens.push(fcmToken.token);
            }
          }
          if (tokens.length > 0) {
            return admin
              .messaging()
              .sendToDevice(tokens, payload)
```

```
            .then(response => {
              const tokensToRemove = [];
              response.results.forEach((result, index) => {
                const error = result.error;
                if (error) {
                  console.error(
                    'Failure sending notification to',
                    tokens[index],
                    error
                  );
                  if (
                    error.code === 'messaging/invalid-registration-token'
||
                    error.code ===
                      'messaging/registration-token-not-registered'
                  ) {
                    tokensToRemove.push(
                      allTokens.ref.child(tokens[index]).remove()
                    );
                  }
                }
              });
              return Promise.all(tokensToRemove);
            });
          }
        }
      });
    });
```

# Testing our push notifications

Run **yarn deploy**, and then we can test out our push notifications.

The easiest way to test it is to simply open up a tab of our deployed app, and then another version in an **Incognito** tab (using Chrome). Log in to each tab with different users, and when you send a message, you should see the following:

Note that you must not have both tabs in focus; you need to open both tabs, but switch away from one, otherwise the notification won't display.

# Debugging push notifications

If you encounter any problems, you can try the following steps.

## Checking the Cloud Functions logs

After you log in to `console.firebase.com`, under the **Functions** tab, there's a log tab that shows the execution of each function. Any errors will show up here and also, any of the old token deletions we configured. Check to ensure that A) the function is actually running when you send a message and B) there are no errors that interfere with the sending.

## Checking the Service Worker

As we said earlier, the Service Worker should update given any byte-difference in its size as well as after every reload if **Update on reload** is checked in **Chrome DevTools | Application**. However, even with those steps, I found that the service worker often did not actually update on redeployment. If you're having problems, click on **Unregister** beside each instance under the **Application | Service Workers** tab of DevTools. Then, click on the name of each service worker file to ensure that the code matches what's in your `build` folder.

## Checking the tokens

Ensure that the tokens are saving and updating correctly in the database. There should be no duplicates with different user IDs.

# Summary

Push notifications are tricky. In this chapter, we had to write a lot of code with very few benchmarks to check in along the way. If you're running into problems, ensure that all your code matches the examples.

Once your notifications are working, though, we'll have bridged a major gap between web apps and native applications. Now, it's time to take another step into the world of native apps, by making our apps installable by the user.

# 9
# Making Our App Installable with a Manifest

We're now starting down the road to Progressive Web App land. From now on, our only focus will be on taking our existing application and making it faster, sleeker, and more user-friendly.

One of the big advantages of the Progressive Web App is bridging the gap between a web application (viewed in a browser) and a native app (launched as a separate application). The next few chapters, in particular, will focus on making our web app more native-like, without losing all the advantages of a web application.

The first major benefit of a web application over a native app is the lack of an install barrier. If you create a native app, you need to convince users to devote precious storage and bandwidth, before they even use your application. They must be willing to sit through the download and install process. Then they have to keep it around, even if they don't use it that often.

Web applications have no such barrier. You can use them almost instantly, and the most sophisticated web apps have functionality that rivals native apps. What's their disadvantage? Well, the user has to navigate to their browser, then to the web page, in order to use it. They don't have the nice tidy reminder of the app's existence staring at them from their phone's home screen.

What would the best of both worlds be? It would be an application that allows user to try it out before they commit to installing it to their device, but once it's installed, it acts exactly like a native application, with an icon on the device's home screen.

How can we achieve this? We can do so with a web app manifest.

In this chapter, we'll cover the following:

- What is a web app manifest?
- How to make our app installable on Android
- How to make our app installable on iOS
- Using web app install banners

# What is an app manifest?

In `Chapter 2`, *Getting Started with Webpack,* when we set up our Webpack build configuration, we ensured that our build process generated an asset manifest, with the filename `asset-manifest.json`.

This file contains a list of the JavaScript files our application uses. If we want to, we can configure it to also list the CSS and image files we use.

This asset manifest gives us an idea of what manifests are used for--describing some part of application. Our web app manifest is similar, but simply describes what our application is all about from a higher level, in a way that resembles an App Store description of a native app.

That's what it looks like, and we'll dive more into that soon as we build out our file, but the real magic of the web app manifest is what it does.

On some browsers (more on that later in the chapter), if your web application includes a proper web app manifest, the user can choose to save the web page to their home screen, where it will appear like a regular app, with its own launch icon. When they click on the icon, it will launch with a splash screen and (though it's running from the browser) run in full screen mode, so it looks and feels like a regular app.

# Browser support

Here's the downside of the web app manifest--it's a new technology. As such, few browsers actually support it. As of now, only newer versions of Android Webview and Chrome for Android have full support.

I'm predicting that support will come soon to all newer browsers, but where does that leave us for the moment?

In short, there are ways to activate similar functionality on older browsers. In this chapter, we'll cover using a web app manifest (for those of you on newer browsers, and to prepare you for the future) and a **polyfill** for iOS devices.

If you're interested in covering other devices, there are polyfills available, such as **ManUp** (`https://github.com/boyofgreen/manUp.js/`). What these polyfills do is that they take the gamut of workarounds for different devices and compile them into one manifest file.

However, this book is about the future of web applications, so we'll show you everything you need to prepare for the world of web app manifests.

# Making our app installable - Android

Google is one of the biggest proponents of PWA's, so it makes sense that their Chrome browser and Android operating system are the most friendly to web app manifests.

Let's go through the process of creating a manifest in a way that makes it work with the latest version of Chrome. Later in this chapter, we'll go through the same process in a more manual way in order to support iOS.

# Manifest properties

Let's get to it! In your `public/` folder, create a file called `manifest.json`, and then add an empty object. Each of the following will be a key-value pair of that object. We'll take a quick tour through each of the available properties:

- `name`: Your application's name. Simple!:

    ```
    "name": "Chatastrophe",
    ```

- `short_name`: A human readable version of your application's name. This is for times when the full name won't fit, like on your user's home screen. If your app's name is "Why PWAs Are Great For Everyone", you can shorten it to "PWAs R Great" or something here:

    ```
    "short_name": "Chatastrophe",
    ```

- `icons`: A list of icons for the user's device to use. We will just use our current logo, which is conveniently the maximum size needed for an icon.
  Google recommends the following set of icons:

    - 128x128 as a base icon size
    - 152x152 for Apple devices
    - 144x144 for Microsoft devices
    - 192x192 for Chrome
    - 256x256, 384x384, and 512x512 for different device sizes

  The last two are included in the asset bundle. We'll need our designers to create the rest for our production build, but they're not needed just yet:

```
"icons": [
  {
    "src":"/assets/icon.png",
    "sizes": "192x192",
    "type": "image/png"
  },
  {
    "src": "/assets/icon-256.png",
    "sizes": "256x256",
    "type": "image/png"
  },
  {
    "src": "/assets/icon-384.png",
    "sizes": "384x384",
    "type": "image/png"
  },
  {
    "src": "/assets/icon-512.png",
    "sizes": "512x512",
    "type": "image/png"
  }
],
```

- `start_url`: The Start URL is used for analytics purposes so that you can see how many users are visiting your web application via an installed PWA. It's optional, but doesn't hurt:

```
"start_url": "/?utm_source=homescreen",
```

- `background_color`: The background color is used for the color of the splash screen that displays when our application starts up. Here, we set it to a nice orange-red:

  ```
  "background_color": "#e05a47",
  ```

- `theme_color`: This is similar to `background_color`, but it styles the toolbar on Android when your app is active. A nice touch:

  ```
  "theme_color": "#e05a47",
  ```

- `display`: As we said earlier, PWAs can be launched as if they were a native app, AKA the browser bar is hidden; that's what this property activates. You can set it to "browser" if you think it'd be better for your users to be able to see the address bar:

  ```
  "display": "standalone"
  ```

# Other properties

There are a few more properties you need to be aware of for our app:

- `related_applications`: You can provide a list of native applications related to your web application, with a URL to download; pair it with `prefer_related_applications`.
- `prefer_related_applications`: A boolean that defaults to false. If true, the user will be notified about the related applications.
- `scope`: A string, such as `/app`. If the user navigates to a page outside the scope, the app will return to the appearance of a regular web page in the browser.
- `description`: A description of what your app does; not mandatory.
- `dir`: The direction of the type.
- `lang`: The language of the `short_name`. When paired with `dir`, can be used to ensure that right to left languages display correctly.

# Linking our manifest

That's it! At the end, your `manifest.json` should look like this:

```json
{
  "name": "Chatastrophe",
  "short_name": "Chatastrophe",
  "icons": [
    {
      "src":"/assets/icon.png",
      "sizes": "192x192",
      "type": "image/png"
    },
    {
      "src": "/assets/icon-256.png",
      "sizes": "256x256",
      "type": "image/png"
    },
    {
      "src": "/assets/icon-384.png",
      "sizes": "384x384",
      "type": "image/png"
    },
    {
      "src": "/assets/icon-512.png",
      "sizes": "512x512",
      "type": "image/png"
    }
  ],
  "start_url": "/?utm_source=homescreen",
  "background_color": "#e05a47",
  "theme_color": "#e05a47",
  "display": "standalone"
}
```

You can then link it from your `index.html`, as shown:

```html
<link rel="manifest" href="/manifest.json">
```

Ensure that you also copy it into your `build` folder.

If all went well, and you have the latest version of Chrome, you can check whether it worked properly by going to the `Application` tab in Chrome Dev Tools. Ensure that you restart your server first. You should see the following:

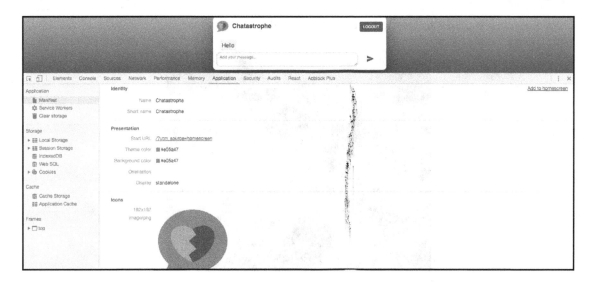

Now to test it! Let's run our deploy process again with `yarn deploy`. When that's done, navigate to the application on your Android device. In order to trigger the web app install banner, you need to visit the site twice, with five minutes between visits:

If you don't see the install banner, you can also install it by going to the options dropdown and selecting **Add to Home Screen**.

Once you click on **Add to Home Screen**, you should see it appear:

Then, when we launch, we get a beautiful splash screen:

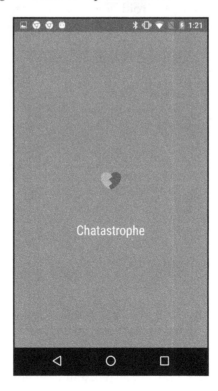

It's lovely.

That's the gist of making an installable PWA for Android. It's a nice and streamlined process, thanks to Google's advocacy of PWAs, but many of our users will undoubtedly be using iPhones, so we have to ensure that we support them as well.

# Making our app installable - iOS

Apple hasn't come out in support of Progressive Web Apps, as of the time of writing. There's numerous theories as to why (their revenue-generating App Store ecosystem, competition with Google, lack of control), but it does mean that the process of making our app installable is much more manual.

Let's be clear--the optimal PWA experience, as of now, will be for a user on the latest version of Chrome, on an Android device.

However, PWAs are also all about progressive enhancement, a concept we'll cover in more depth in the later chapters. Progressive enhancement means we deliver the best possible experience for each user on their device; if they can support all the shiny new stuff, great, otherwise, we do our best with the tools they are using.

So, let's go through the process of making our UX delightful for an iPhone user who wants to save our app to their home screen.

We'll use lots of <meta> tags to tell the browser that our app is installable. Let's start with the icon:

```
<link rel="apple-touch-icon" href="/assets/icon.png">
```

Add the following to `public/index.html` (for the rest of this section, group all your `meta` tags above your `link` tags). This defines what the icon will be on the user's home screen.

Next, we add a title to our page, which will be used as the name of the app on the home screen. Add this after your `link` tags:

```
<title>Chatastrophe</title>
```

Then, we need to let iOS know that this is a web app. You can do so with the following `meta` tag:

```
<meta name="apple-mobile-web-app-capable" content="yes">
```

As we did with `theme_color` in the Android section, we want to style the way the status bar appears. The default value is black, which looks like this:

The other option is black-translucent, which is not very black, and mainly translucent:

Add this with the following:

```
<meta name="apple-mobile-web-app-status-bar-style" content="black-
translucent">
```

The last thing we want to do is style the splash screen; what appears as the app boots up.

The way to do this on iOS is a little manual--you provide a static image.

For full support, you need to provide a separate startup image for each iOS screen size, from iPads to the smallest iPhone. If you want to see a great example of multiple startup images and icons, check the gist at `https://gist.github.com/tfausak/2222823`. Included here are the startup image links from that gist:

```
<!-- iPad retina portrait startup image -->
<link href="https://placehold.it/1536x2008"
      media="(device-width: 768px) and (device-height: 1024px)
             and (-webkit-device-pixel-ratio: 2)
             and (orientation: portrait)"
      rel="apple-touch-startup-image">

<!-- iPad retina landscape startup image -->
<link href="https://placehold.it/1496x2048"
      media="(device-width: 768px) and (device-height: 1024px)
             and (-webkit-device-pixel-ratio: 2)
             and (orientation: landscape)"
      rel="apple-touch-startup-image">

<!-- iPad non-retina portrait startup image -->
<link href="https://placehold.it/768x1004"
      media="(device-width: 768px) and (device-height: 1024px)
             and (-webkit-device-pixel-ratio: 1)
             and (orientation: portrait)"
      rel="apple-touch-startup-image">

<!-- iPad non-retina landscape startup image -->
<link href="https://placehold.it/748x1024"
      media="(device-width: 768px) and (device-height: 1024px)
             and (-webkit-device-pixel-ratio: 1)
             and (orientation: landscape)"
      rel="apple-touch-startup-image">

<!-- iPhone 6 Plus portrait startup image -->
<link href="https://placehold.it/1242x2148"
      media="(device-width: 414px) and (device-height: 736px)
             and (-webkit-device-pixel-ratio: 3)
             and (orientation: portrait)"
      rel="apple-touch-startup-image">

<!-- iPhone 6 Plus landscape startup image -->
<link href="https://placehold.it/1182x2208"
      media="(device-width: 414px) and (device-height: 736px)
             and (-webkit-device-pixel-ratio: 3)
             and (orientation: landscape)"
      rel="apple-touch-startup-image">

<!-- iPhone 6 startup image -->
```

```
<link href="https://placehold.it/750x1294"
      media="(device-width: 375px) and (device-height: 667px)
            and (-webkit-device-pixel-ratio: 2)"
      rel="apple-touch-startup-image">

<!-- iPhone 5 startup image -->
<link href="https://placehold.it/640x1096"
      media="(device-width: 320px) and (device-height: 568px)
            and (-webkit-device-pixel-ratio: 2)"
      rel="apple-touch-startup-image">

<!-- iPhone < 5 retina startup image -->
<link href="https://placehold.it/640x920"
      media="(device-width: 320px) and (device-height: 480px)
            and (-webkit-device-pixel-ratio: 2)"
      rel="apple-touch-startup-image">

<!-- iPhone < 5 non-retina startup image -->
<link href="https://placehold.it/320x460"
      media="(device-width: 320px) and (device-height: 480px)
            and (-webkit-device-pixel-ratio: 1)"
      rel="apple-touch-startup-image">
```

You may note that these links do not include any iPhone later than the iPhone 6 Plus. As of the time of writing, startup images have questionable support on iOS 9, and no support on iOS 10. While this doesn't detract from the user experience of your app (splash screens should only be seen for a second, anyway) it's an indicator of Apple's lack of full support for PWAs. Hopefully, this will change in the near future.

Overall, making your app an installable web app for iOS is not as fancy or intuitive as a `manifest.json`, but fairly straightforward. Redeploy your app with `yarn deploy`, and then open the web page with Safari on your iPhone. Then, hit share and **Add to Home Screen**:

It should appear on your home screen just like a regular app and, when launched, appear like this:

This is very slick.

Here's what the final index.html should look like:

```
<!DOCTYPE html>
<html lang="en">
  <head>
    <meta name="viewport" content="width=device-width, initial-scale=1">
    <meta charset="utf-8">
    <meta name="apple-mobile-web-app-capable" content="yes">
    <meta name="apple-mobile-web-app-status-bar-style" content="black-
translucent">
    <link rel="shortcut icon" href="assets/favicon.ico" type="image/x-
icon">
    <link rel="manifest" href="/manifest.json">
```

```
    <link rel="apple-touch-icon" href="/assets/icon.png">
    <title>Chatastrophe</title>
  </head>
  <body>
    <div id="root"></div>
    <script src="/secrets.js"></script>
    <script
src="https://www.gstatic.com/firebasejs/4.3.0/firebase.js"></script>
    <script>
      // Initialize Firebase
      var config = {
        apiKey: window.apiKey,
        authDomain: "chatastrophe-draft.firebaseapp.com",
        databaseURL: "https://chatastrophe-draft.firebaseio.com",
        projectId: "chatastrophe-draft",
        storageBucket: "chatastrophe-draft.appspot.com",
        messagingSenderId: window.messagingSenderId
      };
      window.firebase = firebase;
      firebase.initializeApp(config);
    </script>
  </body>
</html>
```

# App install banners and you

Being able to add to home screen is great functionality, but how will our user know that our application is installable, especially if they've never heard of PWAs?

Enter the **Web App Install Banner**. Previously, App Install Banners were a handy way to advertise your native app--see the following example from Flipboard:

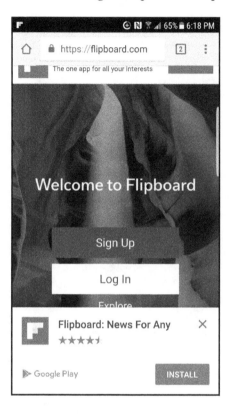

Now, however, Google is leading the charge on PWA install banners, prompting the user to add to home screen. See the following example from the Chrome Dev Summit site:

This banner has the advantages of making your users aware that your site is a PWA, and for those unfamiliar with installable web apps, providing an entry point into the world of PWAs.

Here's what it looks like on your home screen when you click on **Add** in the preceding screenshot:

However, like everything in this section, this is new technology. As of now, firm support only exists on Chrome on Android and Opera for Android. Furthermore, there are firm criteria for when the install banner will appear on both browsers:

- The app must have a web app manifest
- The app must be served over HTTPS
- The app must use a service worker
- The app must be visited twice, with at least five minutes between the visits

We have covered the first three (Firebase apps are automatically deployed over HTTPS). The last criterion is to minimize annoyance on the part of the user.

# Delaying the app install banner

 The following section is only applicable if you have an Android device to test on, with the latest version of Chrome or Opera for Android. You'll also need to set up Remote Debugging for your Android device, following the guide at `https://developers.google.com/web/tools/chrome-devtools/remote-debugging/`.

One of the advantages of PWAs that we cited earlier is the fact that the user gets a chance to interact with your application before deciding whether to install. Web app install banners can possibly disrupt that process if they display too early (before the user has had a positive interaction with your application).

In this section, we'll find a way around that by delaying the web app install banner event until the user has a positive interaction with our application.

We will add an event listener to our `App.js`, to listen for when the banner display event is ready to fire. Then, we'll intercept that event, and save it for when the user sends a message.

## Listening for the event

Chrome emits the `beforeinstallprompt` event directly before it displays the web app install banner. That's the event we will listen to. Like our other Firebase event listeners, let's add this to our `App.js` `componentDidMount`.

We'll create a method called `listenForInstallBanner`, and then call that method from within `componentDidMount`:

```
componentDidMount() {
  firebase.auth().onAuthStateChanged(user => {
    if (user) {
      this.setState({ user });
    } else {
      this.props.history.push('/login');
    }
  });
  firebase
    .database()
    .ref('/messages')
    .on('value', snapshot => {
      this.onMessage(snapshot);
      if (!this.state.messagesLoaded) {
        this.setState({ messagesLoaded: true });
```

```
      }
    });
    this.listenForInstallBanner();
  }

  listenForInstallBanner = () => {

  };
```

Within `listenForInstallBanner`, we will do two things:

1. Register a listener for the event.
2. When that event fires, cancel it and store it for later.

Storing it for later means we trigger it whenever we please, AKA when the user sends their first message.

Here's what the code looks like:

```
  listenForInstallBanner = () => {
    window.addEventListener('beforeinstallprompt', (e) => {
      console.log('beforeinstallprompt Event fired');
      e.preventDefault();
      // Stash the event so it can be triggered later.
      this.deferredPrompt = e;
    });
  };
```

We're storing our `deferredPrompt` on the `App` instance, so we can grab it later. Which we'll do, instead our `handleSubmitMessage` method:

```
  handleSubmitMessage = msg => {
    const data = {
      msg,
      author: this.state.user.email,
      user_id: this.state.user.uid,
      timestamp: Date.now()
    };
    firebase
      .database()
      .ref('messages/')
      .push(data);
    if (this.deferredPrompt) {
      this.deferredPrompt.prompt();
      this.deferredPrompt.userChoice.then(choice => {
        console.log(choice);
      });
```

```
        this.deferredPrompt = null;
    }
};
```

After we submit our message, we trigger our saved event. Then, we log out the user choice (whether or not they actually install the app, which we can also send to whatever analytics we choose to use in the future). Lastly, we delete the event.

Okay, let's test this!

Plug your Android device into your computer, and open up remote debugging on the DevTools. We'll have to deploy our app first, so hit `yarn deploy` and wait for it to finish. Then, open up the application on your device and type a message; you should see the app install banner pop up.

If it doesn't appear, check your code, or go to the **Application** tab of DevTools and click on the **Add to Home Screen** button. This should trigger the `beforeinstallprompt` event.

# Summary

Web app install banners are still a new technology, and the standards are in a state of flux. For the latest information, consult Google's page on web app install banners--`https://developers.google.com/web/fundamentals/engage-and-retain/app-install-banners/`. That said, I hope this chapter was helpful in illuminating the possibilities of the banners, and the current state of the technology.

Now that we've made our app bigger and better, it's time to slim down, and focus purely on performance. See you in the next chapter!

# 10
# The App Shell

Our last chapter was about adding home screen installation and push notifications--both meant to improve the user's experience by adding functionality--but, as we described in our user stories at the beginning of the book, one of the most important features of this app was its inclusiveness; it was a chat app for everyone, anyone, anywhere.

From a web app perspective, we can better rephrase that as "any connection, any speed." The biggest blocker of web application performance is network requests: how long it takes to load data over a poor connection.

Developers can fail to give performance its due attention, simply because we usually test our sites on speedy connections inside air-conditioned buildings in urban hubs. However, for a global app such as Chatastrophe, we must think about the users in less developed countries, the users in rural areas, and the users who only have a tenth of the network speed we do. How can we make the app work for them?

This section is all about performance; specifically, it's about optimizing our app so that it performs well even in the worst conditions. If we do it well, we'll have a robust user experience, suited for any speed (or lack thereof).

In this chapter, we'll cover these things:

- What progressive enhancement is
- The RAIL model of performance
- Using Chrome DevTools to measure performance
- Moving our app shell out of React

# What is progressive enhancement?

**Progressive enhancement** is a simple idea with big consequences. It comes from a desire to provide an awesome user experience, married with the need for performance. If all our users had perfect, ultrafast connections, we could build an incredible application. However, if all our users have slow connections, we have to settle for a more bare-bones experience.

Progressive enhancement says porque no los dos? Why not both?

Our audience includes both fast connections and slow connections. We should serve both, and serve each appropriately, which means providing the best experience for the best connections and a more stripped-down (but still great) experience for poor connections, and everything in between.

In a sentence, progressive enhancement means our application gets progressively better as our user's connection improves, but it is always useful and useable. Our application is thus an application adaptive to the connection.

You can actually imagine that this as exactly how a modern web page loads. First, we load the HTML--the basic, ugly skeleton of our content. Then, we add the CSS to make it pretty. Lastly, we load the JavaScript, which contains all the good stuff to make it pop. In other words, our application gets progressively better as the site loads.

The progressive enhancement paradigms urge us to reorganize our site's content so that the importance stuff loads as quickly as possible, and then the bells and whistles come in. So, if you're on a super fast connection, you get everything, now; otherwise, you get just what you need to get using the application and the rest of the stuff comes later.

So, in this chapter, we'll optimize our application to boot up as quickly as possible. We'll also cover many tools you can use to keep an eye on performance, and continually enhance it, but how do we measure performance? What metrics can we use to ensure that we're delivering a fast app? Enter the RAIL model.

# The RAIL model

RAIL is what Google calls a "user-centric performance model". It's a set of guidelines for measuring our app's performance. We should try to avoid straying outside of these suggestions.

We will use RAIL's principles to speed up our application and ensure that it performs well enough for all users. You can read Google's full docs on RAIL at `https://developers.google.com/web/fundamentals/performance/rail`.

RAIL outlines four specific periods in an application's life cycle. They are as follows:

- Response
- Animation
- Idle
- Load

Personally, I think it's easier to think about them in reverse order (since it's more true to their actual order), but that would have spelled LIAR, so we can see why Google shied away from that. Either way, that's how we'll cover them here.

# Load

First, your application loads (let there be light!).

RAIL says that the optimal load time is one second (or less). That doesn't mean your entire application loads in one second; it means the user sees content within one second. They get some sense that the current task (loading the page) is progressing in a meaningful way, rather than staring at a blank white screen. As we'll see, this is easier said than done!

# Idle

Once your application is done loading, it is idle (and also will be idle between actions) until a user performs an action.

Rather than letting your app just sit there (being lazy!), RAIL argues that we should use this time to continue loading in parts of the application.

We'll see this more in the next chapter, but if our initial load is just the bare bones version of our app, we load the rest (progressive enhancement!) during idle time.

# Animation

Animation will be less relevant to our purpose, but we'll cover it briefly here. Essentially, users will note a lag in animations if they are not performed at 60 fps. This will negatively affect the perceived performance (how the user feels about your app's speed).

Note that RAIL also defines scrolling and touch gestures as animations, so even if you have no animations, if your scroll is laggy, you have a problem.

# Response

Eventually (hopefully very quickly!), the user performs an action. Usually, that will mean clicking on a button or typing or using a gesture. Once they do so, you have 100 ms to provide a response that acknowledges their action; otherwise, users will notice and get frustrated, and maybe retry the action, causing more problems down the line (we've all experienced this--the mad double- and triple-clicking).

Note that some actions will take longer to complete, if you need to do some calculation or network requests. You don't need to complete the action in 100 ms, but you do have to provide some response; otherwise, as *Meggin Kearney* puts it, "the connection between action and reaction is broken. Users will notice."

# Timeline

As the preceding model illustrates, there are certain time limitations, within which our application has to live. Here's a handy reference:

- >16ms: Time per frame of any animation/scrolling.
- >100ms: Response to user action.
- >1000ms: Display content on the web page.
- 1000ms+: User loses focus.
- 10,000ms+: User will likely abandon the page.

If your application performs according to these specifications, you're in good standing (and these are not easy to do, as we shall see).

# Measuring using the timeline

In this section, we'll look at how to profile our application's performance using the Chrome DevTools, the first of a few tools we'll use to track how our application loads and responds.

Once we have an idea of how it performs, we can improve it according to RAIL principles.

The DevTools are, of course, always under development, so their appearance may differ from the given screenshots. The core functionality should remain the same, however, and so, it's important to pay close attention to the principles at work.

Go to your deployed Firebase application in Chrome and open up DevTools to the **Performance** tab (I recommend undocking the tools into a separate window via the dropdown menu in the top right, since there's a lot of content to see); then, refresh the page. After the page finishes loading, you should see something similar to the following:

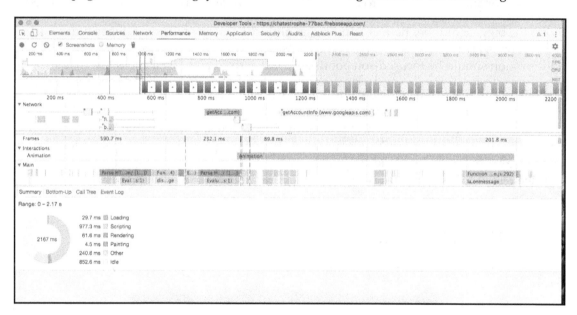

There's a lot going on here, so let's break it down. We'll start with the **Summary** tab, the circle graph at the bottom there.

# The Summary tab

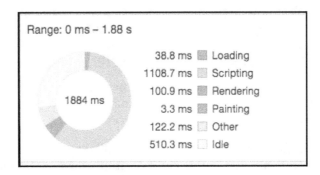

The number in the middle is how long it took for our application to fully complete loading. Your number should be similar to mine, with some variation based on your internet speed.

By far the biggest number here is scripting, at almost 1000 ms on its own. Since our application is JavaScript-heavy, this makes sense. Right away, we can see where most of our optimization should be focused--on booting up our scripting as fast as possible.

The other significant number is the amount of idle time (almost as much as scripting time). We'll see why there's so much in a moment, but keep in mind that the RAIL model recommends using that time to start preloading bits of the application that haven't loaded yet. As of now, we load everything at the start, boot it all up, and then sit around for a bit. It will make far more sense to load only what we need (thus reducing scripting time) and then load the rest in the background (thus reducing idle time).

# Network requests

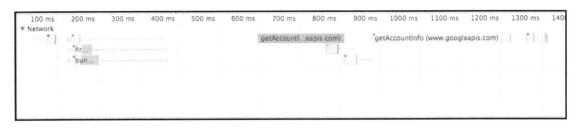

We will jump up to network requests now, since it'll help explain a lot of the rest of the performance profile.

Here, you can see what data was exactly loaded in at what time. At the beginning, we see a lot of the setup files: the Firebase app and `messaging` libraries, our `bundle.js`, and the actual document for the page.

Later on, the two significant calls are for the user: to log in and load the user details. The last thing we load is the manifest.

This ordering makes sense. We need to load the Firebase libraries and our JavaScript in order to boot up our application. Once we do so, we start the login process.

The next thing that happens, once our user logs in, is that we receive the messages, data from Firebase. As you'll note, this does not show up on the chart, because it's done over WebSockets, in real time, so it's not a network request as such. However, it will figure into the rest of the performance profile, so keep it in mind.

# Waterfall

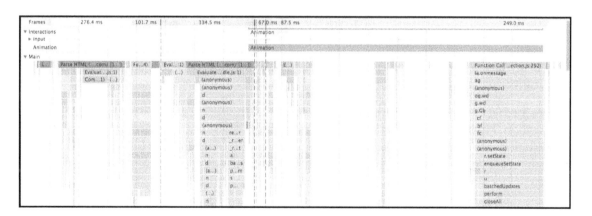

Here, we have a detailed breakdown of what Chrome is actually doing at any time during the rendering process.

The Waterfall tool is detailed and complex, so we'll have to be content with a surface glimpse here. There are two insights we can draw just from looking at it, however. First, we can see all the idle time visualized. Most of it is at the start, which is somewhat unavoidable as we first load the document, but there's that great gap in the middle that we can try to fill.

Second, you can see when the application receives the messages from Firebase, in the rightmost waterfall section. If you hover over each block, you can actually trace Firebase receiving the message down to our App.js, setting its state to the messages array.

So, while we can't see the messages loading in the network request, we can see the response in the JavaScript execution.

# Screenshots

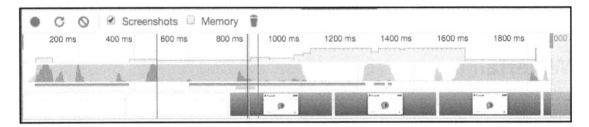

This is my favorite section of the **Performance** Tools, because it vividly illustrates how your application loads.

As we established earlier, users should see content within 1,000 ms of loading your application. Here, we can see that content first appears on our application at about 400 ms, so we're looking good, but as our application grows (and our scripting burden increases) that may change, so now's the time to optimize as much as possible.

# PageSpeed Insights

The **Performance** Tools are great in that they let us dive deep into the nitty gritty of our application's loading. We will use them to keep track of our app's performance as we try to improve it, but, if we want more specific, detailed suggestions, we can turn to **PageSpeed Insights**, a tool provided by Google.

Go to PageSpeed Insights (`https://developers.google.com/speed/pagespeed/insights/`) and plug in the URL of your deployed application. After a few seconds, you'll get recommendations about what can we improve about Chatastrophe:

As you can see, our mobile performance is in dire need of aid. Most of the insights focus on our render-blocking JavaScript and CSS. I encourage you to read through their descriptions of these problems and try fixing them on your own. In the next section, we'll work on improving our app to Google's specifications, using another Progressive Web App secret weapon--the app shell pattern.

# The app shell pattern

The essence of our application is the message list and chat box, where users read and write messages.

This core functionality relies on JavaScript to work. We cannot get around the fact that we are unable to display the messages until the user has been authenticated through Firebase and the messages array has loaded, but everything surrounding those two pieces is mostly static content. It's the same in every view and it does not rely on JavaScript to work:

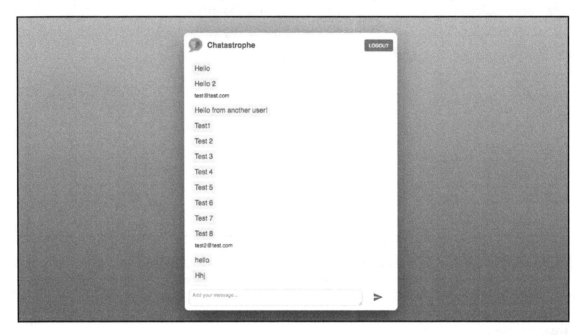

We can refer to this as the application shell--the frame around the functional, JavaScript driven core.

Since this frame does not rely on JavaScript to function, there's actually no need for us to wait for React to load and boot up all our JavaScript before displaying it—which is what is currently happening.

Right now, our shell is a part of our React code, so, all our JavaScript has to be loaded before we call `ReactDOM.render` and display it on the screen.

However, with our app, and with many apps, there's a significant section of the UI that is essentially just HTML and CSS. Also, if our goal is to decrease perceived load time (how long the user thinks it takes to load our app) and get content on the screen as soon as possible, we're better off keeping our shell just as HTML and CSS, that is, separating it from our JavaScript so that we don't have to wait for React.

Going back to our **Performance** Tools, you can see that the first thing loaded is the document, or our `index.html`:

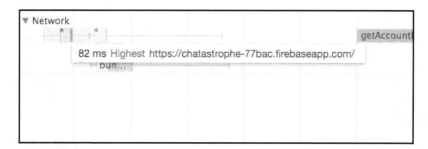

If we can move our shell in that `index.html`, it'll appear a heck of a lot faster than it currently is, because it won't have to wait for the bundle to load.

Before we begin, however, let's take a benchmark to see where we are and how much of an improvement this will make.

Using your deployed app, open up our **Performance** Tools and refresh the application (use the **Empty Cache & Hard Reload** option available when DevTools is open to ensure that there's no accidental caching going on—hold and press the reload button to access it). Then, take a look at that image strip and see when content first appears:

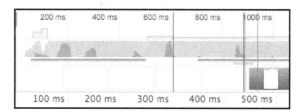

Run the test three times, to be sure, and then take the average. For me, it took an average of 600 ms. That's our benchmark to beat.

# Moving shell HTML out of React

Let's start by defining what we want to move into our `index.html`.

In the following image, everything outside the messages and chat box line is our app shell:

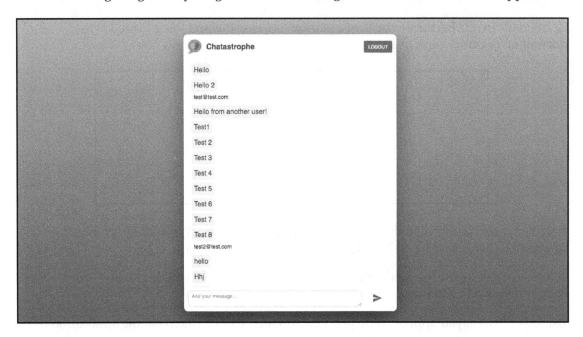

That's what we want to move out of React and convert to plain HTML, but let's clarify something before moving on.

Our goal here is to create a fast-loading version of the parts of our app that don't need JavaScript immediately but, ultimately, some of our shell will need JavaScript. We need our logout button in the header and that will need JavaScript to function (though only once the user is authenticated).

So, while we talk of moving this content out of React, what we'll actually do is have a pure HTML and CSS version of the shell and then, when React initializes, we will replace it with with the React version.

This approach gives us the best of both worlds: a fast-loading version of the basics, which we'll swap out once the JS is ready. If this sounds familiar, you can also call it progressively enhancing our app.

So, how can we manage this swap-out? Well, let's start by opening our `index.html` and taking a look at how our application initializes:

```
</head>
<body>
  <div id="root"></div>
  <script src="/secrets.js"></script>
  <script src="https://www.gstatic.com/firebasejs/4.1.2/firebase.js"></script>
  <script>
    // Initialize Firebase
    var config = {
      apiKey: window.apiKey,
      authDomain: "chatastrophe-77bac.firebaseapp.com",
      databaseURL: "https://chatastrophe-77bac.firebaseio.com",
```

The key is our `div#root`. As we see in our `index.js`, that's where we inject our React content:

```
ReactDOM.render(
  <BrowserRouter>
    <App />
  </BrowserRouter>,
  document.getElementById('root')
);
```

Right now, we're embedding our React content into an empty `div`, but let's try out something; add an `<h1>` in there:

```
<div id="root">
  <h1>Hello</h1>
</div>
```

Then, reload your app:

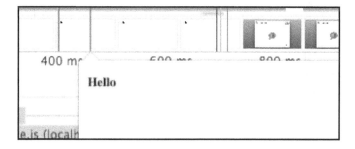

The `<h1>` appears until our React is ready, in which case it is replaced, so we can add content inside `div#root` and it'll simply be overwritten when React is ready; that's our key.

Let's progressively move content over, starting from our `App.js` and working our way downward:

```
render() {
  return (
    <div id="container">
      <Route path="/login" component={LoginContainer} />
      <Route exact path="/" render={() => (
        <ChatContainer
          messagesLoaded={this.state.messagesLoaded}
          onSubmit={this.handleSubmitMessage}
          messages={this.state.messages}
          user={this.state.user} />
      )} />
      <Route path="/users/:id" render={({ history, match }) => (
        <UserContainer
          messages={this.state.messages}
          messagesLoaded={this.state.messagesLoaded}
          userID={match.params.id}/>
      )} />
    </div>
  )
}
```

The only bit of HTML (or JSX, currently) we need here is the container. Let's copy that into `div#root`:

```
<div id="root">
  <div id="container">
  </div>
</div>
```

Then, inside `ChatContainer` (or `LoginContainer`, or `UserContainer`), we see we have a `div.inner-container`, which also can be moved over:

```
<div id="root">
  <div id="container">
    <div class="inner-container">
    </div>
  </div>
</div>
```

 Note the change from `className` (for JSX) to `class` (for HTML).

Then, we move the `Header` itself:

```
<div id="root">
  <div id="container">
    <div class="inner-container">
      <div id="Header">
        <img src="/assets/icon.png" alt="logo" />
        <h1>Chatastrophe</h1>
      </div>
    </div>
  </div>
</div>
```

Reload your app and you'll see a very ugly version of our HTML appear before the React loads:

What's going on here? Well, our CSS is loaded inside our `App.js`, in our import statements, so it's not ready until our React is. The next step will be to move the relevant CSS inside our `index.html`.

# Moving CSS out of React

Right now, our app doesn't have that much CSS, so we can, in theory, just `<link>` our entire style sheet inside `index.html`, instead of importing it in `App.js`, but as our application and our CSS grow in size, that will be less than optimal.

Our best option is to inline the relevant CSS. We start by adding a `<style>` tag to our `<head>`, right below our `<title>` tags.

Then, open up `src/app.css`, and cut (not copy) the CSS within the `/* Start initial styles */` and `/* End Initial styles */` comments.

Put that inside the style tags and reload the app:

The application looks exactly the same! That's the good news; at this stage, there probably isn't a perceptible difference in load time. However, let's deploy and then run our **Performance** tools again:

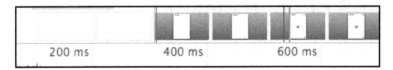

As you can see, the shell (with the blank inner) appears well before the loading indicator appears (a sign that the React app has booted it up). This is time the user will usually spend staring at a blank screen.

# Moving the loading indicator

Let's take it one small step forward, and also add the loading indicator into our app shell, to give the user a sense of what is happening.

Copy the JSX from `ChatContainer` and add it to our `index.html`. Then, reload the page:

```
<div id="root">
  <div id="container">
    <div class="inner-container">
      <div id="Header">
        <img src="/assets/icon.png" alt="logo" />
        <h1>Chatastrophe</h1>
      </div>
      <div id="loading-container">
        <img src="/assets/icon.png" alt="logo" id="loader"/>
      </div>
    </div>
  </div>
</div>
```

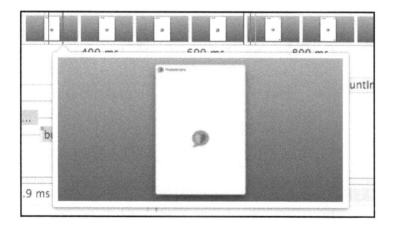

Now, the user gets a clear sense that the application is loading, and will be much more forgiving of our app's load time (though we will still do our best to decrease it).

This is the essential principle to take from this chapter: Progressive Web Apps demand that we do as much as we can to improve our user's experience. Sometimes, we can't do anything about load times (at the end of the day, our JavaScript will always take some time to boot up--and once it does, it provides a great user experience) but we can at least give our user a sense of progress.

Good web design is about empathy. Progressive Web Apps are about being empathetic toward everyone, no matter what conditions they're accessing your app from.

# Summary

In this chapter, we covered the essentials of performance tooling and concepts, from RAIL to DevTools, to PageSpeed Insights. We also made a significant performance improvement using the app shell pattern. We'll continue to hone our app's performance in the following chapters.

Our next chapter will tackle the biggest performance hurdle--our behemoth JavaScript file. We'll learn how to split it into smaller chunks using the magic of React Router and how to load those chunks during the idle time of our app. Let's get to it!

# 11
# Chunking JavaScript to Optimize Performance with Webpack

As we discussed in the last chapter, the biggest problem with converting React applications to Progressive Web Apps is React; more specifically, it's the amount of JavaScript that intrinsically comes along with building a modern JavaScript application. Parsing and running that JavaScript is the biggest single bottleneck for Chatastrophe's performance.

In the last chapter, we took some measures to improve the perceived startup time of our application, by moving content out of our JavaScript and into our `index.html`. While this is a very effective method of displaying content to the user as quickly as possible, you'll note that we didn't do anything to actually change the size of our JavaScript, or reduce the time it takes to initialize all that React goodness.

Well, now's the time to do something about it. In this chapter, we'll look at how we can split up our JavaScript bundle for faster loading. We'll also introduce a new bit of Progressive Web App theory--the PRPL pattern.

In this chapter, we'll cover these topics:

- What is the PRPL pattern?
- What is code splitting and how do we implement it?
- Creating our own higher-order component
- Splitting code by route
- Lazy loading additional routes

# The PRPL pattern

In the last chapter, we introduced some basic principles for performative apps. You want your user to spend as little time as possible waiting, which means loading the essentials as fast as possible and deferring loading the rest of the application to "idle" time for the processor.

These two concepts form the 'I' and 'L' of the RAIL metric. We took a step toward improving the 'L' with the concept of the app shell. Now, we will move some of our 'L' (the initial load) into the 'I' (the idle time of our application) but, before we do that, let's introduce another acronym.

**PRPL** stands for **Push**, **Render**, **Pre-cache**, **Lazy-load**; it's a step-by-step process for how an ideal application should get the content it needs from the server.

Before we dive in, however, I would like to caution the reader that the PRPL pattern is relatively new at the time of writing and may evolve quickly as Progressive Web Apps move into the mainstream. Like many of the concepts we've discussed in this book, it relies on experimental technology only available for certain browsers. This is cutting-edge stuff.

This is how *Addy Osmani* puts it:

> *For most real-world projects, it's frankly too early to realize the PRPL vision in its purest, most complete form, but it's definitely not too early to adopt the mindset, or to start chasing the vision from various angles.* (`https://developers.google.com/web/fundamentals/performance/prpl-pattern/`)

Let's go through each letter in turn and explain what it means for us and our application.

# Push

*Addy Osmani* defines the PUSH of PRPL as follows:

> *"Push critical resources for the initial URL route."*

Essentially, this means that your first priority is loading only what you need to render your initial route as fast as possible. Sound familiar? This is exactly the principle we followed with our application shell.

A gentle definition of Push can be "load the critical content first, before anything else." This definition fits exactly with the app shell pattern, but it's not quite what *Osmani* means.

The following section is a theoretical introduction to server *push* technology. Since we don't have control over our server (AKA Firebase), we won't be implementing this approach, but it's good to know about for your future PWAs that communicate with your own server.

If you look at our `index.html`, you can see that it references several assets. It asks for the `favicon`, the `icon.png`, and `secrets.js`. After Webpack builds, it also requests our main JavaScript `bundle.js`.

How a website normally works is like this: the browser requests `index.html`. Once it gets the file, it goes through and asks the server for all the dependencies listed earlier, each as a separate request.

The core inefficiency here is that `index.html` already contains all the information about its dependencies. In other words, when it responds with `index.html`, the server already "knows" what the browser will request next, so why not anticipate those requests and send all those dependencies along?

Enter HTTP 2.0 Server Push. This technology allows the server to create multiple responses to a single request. The browser asks for `index.html`, and gets `index.html` + `bundle.js` + `icon.png`, and so on.

As *Ilya Grigorik* puts it, Server Push "obsoletes inlining" (`https://www.igvita.com/2013/06/12/innovating-with-http-2.0-server-push/`). No longer do we have to inline our CSS to save trips to the server; we can program our server to send everything we need for our initial route in a single trip. This is exciting stuff; for more information (with a quick tutorial), check out the preceding link.

# Render

After (ideally) pushing all the necessary resources to the client, we render our initial route. Again, we have covered this already, with a fast render, thanks to the app shell pattern.

# Pre-cache

Once we have rendered our initial route, we still have assets required for the other routes. Precaching means that once those assets are loaded, they will go straight into the cache and, if they're requested again, we load them from the cache.

We'll cover this in more detail in the next chapter, as we move into the world of caching.

# Lazy-load

Here's where the meat of this chapter will take place.

We want to load the resources needed for our initial route first, to get that initial rendering done as fast as possible. This means resources needed for other routes will not be loaded.

In practical terms, this means that we want to load `LoginContainer` first (if the user is not logged in) and defer loading `UserContainer`.

However, once that initial route is rendered and the user can see the login screen, we want to prepare for the future. If they then click over to the `UserContainer`, we want to display it as fast as possible. This means loading `UserContainer` resources in the background, once loading the initial route is done.

This process is called **lazy-loading**--loading resources that aren't needed immediately, but may be needed in the future.

The tool we use to do so is code splitting.

# What is code splitting?

**Code splitting** is the act of splitting up our JavaScript file into meaningful chunks in order to improve performance, but why do we need it?

Well, when a user first accesses our application, we only need the JavaScript for the route they're currently on.

This means when they're on `/login`, we only need `LoginContainer.js` and its dependencies. We don't need `UserContainer.js`, so we want to immediately load `LoginContainer.js` and lazy-load `UserContainer.js`. However, our current Webpack setup creates a single `bundle.js` file. All our JavaScript is tied together and must be loaded together. Code splitting is a way to fix that. Instead of a single monolithic JavaScript file, we get multiple JavaScript files, one for each route.

So, we'll get one bundle for `/login`, one for `/user/:id`, and one for `/`. Additionally, we'll get another `main` bundle with all the dependencies.

Whatever route the user visits first, they'll get the bundle for that route and the main bundle. In the background, meanwhile, we'll load the bundles for the other two routes.

Code splitting does not necessarily have to take place on a route-by-route basis, but it makes the most sense for our application. Additionally, code splitting with Webpack and React Router in this way is relatively straightforward to do.

In fact, Webpack will handle this automatically for you, as long as you provide some basic setup. Let's get started with that setup!

# Webpack configuration

Our strategy, as discussed earlier, goes like this: we want to split our `bundle.js` into separate chunks, based on the route.

The purpose of this section is to do two things: one, set up a naming convention for the chunks of JavaScript, and two, add support for conditional imports (more on those soon).

Open up `webpack.config.prod.js` and let's do the first step (this only applies to the `PRODUCTION` build, so only modify our production Webpack config; we don't need code splitting in development).

As it stands, our output configuration looks like this:

```
output: {
    path: __dirname + "/build",
    filename: "bundle.js",
    publicPath: './'
},
```

We create a single JavaScript file in our `build` folder, named `bundle.js`.

Let's change this whole section to the following:

```
output: {
    path: __dirname + "/build",
    filename: 'static/js/[name].[hash:8].js',
    chunkFilename: 'static/js/[name].[hash:8].chunk.js',
    publicPath: './'
},
```

What's going on here?

First, we're moving our JavaScript output to `build/static/js`, just for organization purposes.

Next, we're using two variables in our naming: `name` and `hash`. The name variable is automatically generated by Webpack, using a numbering convention for our chunks. We'll see that in a second.

Then, we use a `hash` variable. Every single time Webpack builds, it generates a new hash--a string of random letters and numbers. We use those to name our files so that each build will have distinct filenames. This will be important in the next chapter because it means our users will never have the issue of the app having been updated, but the cache still holding on to the old files. Since the new files will have new names, they will be downloaded instead of whatever is in the cache.

Next, we're appending a `.chunk` to our code split files (the files for each route). This isn't necessary, but it's recommended if you want to do any special caching with your chunks.

All of the mentioned will make a lot more sense once our code splitting is complete, so let's get there as soon as possible! However, before we move on, we need to add one more thing to our Webpack config.

# Babel stage 1

As we explained in the Webpack chapter, Babel is the tool we use to allow us to use cutting edge JavaScript features and then transpile those into a version of JavaScript the browser will understand.

In this chapter, we will use another cutting edge feature: conditional imports. Before we get started with those, however, we need to change our Babel configuration.

The JavaScript language is constantly evolving. The committee in charge of updating it is called TC39 and they develop updates according to the **TC39 process.** It works as follows:

- A new JavaScript feature is suggested, at which point it is called "stage 0"
- A proposal is created for how it will work ("stage 1")
- An implementation is created ("stage 2")
- It is polished for inclusion ("stage 3")
- It is added to the language

At any point in time, there are multiple features in every stage. The problem is that JavaScript developers are impatient, and any time they hear about a neat feature, they want to start using it, even if it's in stage 3, or 2, or even 0.

Babel provides a way of doing so with its **stage** presets. You can install a preset for each stage and get access to all the features currently in that stage.

The feature we're interested in (conditional imports) is currently in stage 2. In order to use it, we need to install the appropriate babel preset:

```
yarn add --dev babel-preset-stage-2
```

Then, in both Webpack configs, add it under **module | loaders | the JavaScript test | query | presets**:

```
module: {
  loaders: [
  {
  test: /\.js$/,
  exclude: /node_modules/,
  loader: 'babel-loader',
  query: {
        presets: ['es2015','react','stage-2'],
        plugins: ['react-hot-loader/babel', 'transform-class-properties']
      }
  },
```

Remember to add this to both `webpack.config.js` and `webpack.config.prod.js`. We'll need it in both production and development.

# Conditional imports

With that done, it's time to ask what conditional imports are.

Right now, we import all our dependencies at the top of each JavaScript file, as shown:

```
import React, { Component } from 'react';
```

We will always need React, so this import makes sense. It's static, in that it will never change, but the preceding means that React is a dependency of this file and it will always need to be loaded.

Currently, in `App.js`, we do the same with each container:

```
import LoginContainer from './LoginContainer';
import ChatContainer from './ChatContainer';
import UserContainer from './UserContainer';
```

Doing so means that those containers are a dependency of `App.js`, so Webpack will always bundle them together; we can't split them apart.

Instead, we want to import them conditionally, only when we need them.

The mechanism to do so is a little complicated, but it will look as follows, in essence:

```
If (path === '/login')
  import('./LoginContainer')
} else if (path === '/user/:id')
  import('./UserContainer)
} else {
  import('./ChatContainer)
}
```

So, how can we implement this?

# Higher-order components

We discussed higher-order components in `Chapter 5`, *Routing with React*, with the discussion of `withRouter` from React Router; now, we will build one, but first, let's take a quick refresher.

Higher-order components are a fantastically useful pattern in React. If you learn to use them well, you'll open up a whole bunch of possibilities to keep a large code base maintainable and reusable, but they're not as intuitive as regular components, so let's ensure that we cover them well.

At a most basic level, a higher-order component is a function that returns a component.

Imagine that we have a `button` component:

```
function Button(props) {
  return <button color={props.color}>Hello</button>
}
```

This can also be written using `class` syntax, if you're more familiar with that:

```
class Button extends Component {
  render() {
    return <button color={this.props.color}>Hello</button>
  }
}
```

We use a color prop to control the color of the text. Let's say we use this button all over our application. Often, we find ourselves setting the text to red--about 50% of the time.

We can simply continue to pass the `color="red"` prop to our button. This will, in this contrived example, be the superior choice, but we can also make a higher-order component which, in more complex use cases, is the way to go (as we shall see).

Let's create a function called `RedColouredComponent`:

```
function colorRed(Component) {
  return class RedColoredComppnent extends Component {
    render () {
      return <Component color="red" />
    }
  }
}
```

The function takes in a component as an argument. All it does is return a component class, which in turn returns that component with the `color="red"` prop applied.

We can then render our button in another file, as illustrated:

```
import Button from './Button';
import RedColouredComponent from './RedColouredComponent';

const RedButton = RedColouredComponent(Button);

function App() {
 return (
   <div>
     <RedButton />
   </div>
 )
}
```

Then, we can pass any component to `RedColouredComponent` and thus create a red-colored version.

Doing so opens up new worlds of composition--creating components out of combinations of higher-order components.

This is the essence of React, after all--composing UI out of reusable bits of code. Higher order components are a great way to keep our application clean and maintainable, but enough of contrived examples, let's make our own now!

# AsyncComponent

The goal of this section is to create a higher-order component that helps us with code splitting.

This component will only load its dependencies when it is rendered, or when we explicitly tell it to. This means that if we pass it `LoginContainer.js`, it will only load that file when the user navigates to `/login`, or if we tell it to load it.

In other words, this component will give us complete control over when our JavaScript files are loaded and opens up the world of lazy loading. However, it also means that whenever a route is rendered, the relevant files will be automatically loaded.

If that sounds abstract, let's see it in action.

Create a new file in your `components/` directory called `AsyncComponent.js` and add the basic skeleton, as demonstrated:

```
import React, { Component } from 'react'

export default function asyncComponent(getComponent) {

}
```

`asyncComponent` is a function that takes an import statement as an argument, which we call `getComponent`. We know that, as a higher-order component, it will return a component class:

```
export default function asyncComponent(getComponent) {
  return class AsyncComponent extends Component {
    render() {
      return (

      )
    }
  }
}
```

The key for `AsyncComponent` will be the `componentWillMount` life cycle method. This is when `AsyncComponent` will know to go get the dependency file. In this way, the component waits until it is needed, before loading in any files.

However, what do we do with the component after we get it? Simple, store it in state:

```
componentWillMount() {
    if (!this.state.Component) {
        getComponent().then(Component => {
            this.setState({ Component });
        });
    }
}
```

If we have not yet loaded the component, go import it (we'll assume that `getComponent` returns a `Promise`). Once the import is complete, set the state to the imported component, which in turn means our `render` should look like this:

```
render() {
    const { Component } = this.state;
    if (Component) {
        return <Component {...this.props} />;
    }
    return null;
}
```

All this should look familiar to you, except perhaps the `{...this.props}` in the `return` statement. This is the JavaScript spread operator. It's a complicated little thing (more on it at `https://developer.mozilla.org/en-US/docs/Web/JavaScript/Reference/Operators/Spread_operator`) but in this case, it basically means take the `this.props` object and copy all its keys and values onto the `props` of `Component`.

In this way, we can pass props to the component returned by `asyncComponent` and have them passed to the `Component` rendered. Every prop applied to `AsyncComponent` will be applied to the `Component` in its `render` function.

The full component, for reference, is as follows:

```
import React, { Component } from 'react';

export default function asyncComponent(getComponent) {
  return class AsyncComponent extends Component {
    state = { Component: null };

    componentWillMount() {
      if (!this.state.Component) {
        getComponent().then(Component => {
          this.setState({ Component });
        });
      }
    }
  }
```

```
    render() {
      const { Component } = this.state;
      if (Component) {
        return <Component {...this.props} />;
      }
      return null;
    }
  };
}
```

# Route splitting

Let's hop back to App.js, and bring it all together.

First, we'll eliminate App's dependence on the three containers. Replace those imports with an import for AsyncComponent so that the top of the file looks like this:

```
import React, { Component } from 'react';
import { Route, withRouter } from 'react-router-dom';
import AsyncComponent from './AsyncComponent';
import NotificationResource from '../resources/NotificationResource';
import './app.css';
```

Next, we will define three load() functions, one for each container. These are the functions we'll pass to asyncComponent. They must return a promise:

```
const loadLogin = () => {
  return import('./LoginContainer').then(module => module.default);
};

const loadChat = () => {
  return import('./ChatContainer').then(module => module.default);
};

const loadUser = () => {
  return import('./UserContainer').then(module => module.default);
};
```

Behold the magic of conditional imports. When these functions are called, the three JavaScript files will be imported. We then grab the export default from each file and resolve() the Promise with it.

This means we can redefine our components inside App.js, as shown, after the preceding function declarations (which come after the import statements at the top of the file):

```
const LoginContainer = AsyncComponent(loadLogin);
const UserContainer = AsyncComponent(loadUser);
const ChatContainer = AsyncComponent(loadChat);
```

No other changes are necessary! You can keep the app's render statement exactly the same. Now, when we refer to ChatContainer, it refers to the AsyncComponent wrapper around loadChat..., which will go get ChatContainer.js when needed.

Let's see whether it works. Run yarn build, and look at the output:

```
$ node_modules/.bin/webpack --config webpack.config.prod.js
Hash: 2ac9977cd90c3396f070
Version: webpack 2.6.1
Time: 8190ms
                      Asset       Size  Chunks             Chunk Names
static/js/0.2ac9977c.chunk.js    2.88 kB       0  [emitted]
static/js/1.2ac9977c.chunk.js    4.29 kB       1  [emitted]
static/js/2.2ac9977c.chunk.js    4.85 kB       2  [emitted]
   static/js/main.2ac9977c.js      210 kB       3  [emitted]  main
                   index.html    2.82 kB          [emitted]
          asset-manifest.json    249 bytes          [emitted]
```

We have four JavaScript files instead of one. We have our main.js file, which contains App.js plus our necessary node_modules. Then, we have three chunks, one for each container.

Take a look at the file sizes as well and you can see that we didn't gain all too much by this code splitting, a few kilobytes were shed from the main file. However, as our app grows, and each route becomes much more complicated, the benefits of code splitting will scale with it. How easy was that?

# Lazy loading

Lazy loading is the last piece of our PRPL puzzle and is the process of using our application's idle time to load the rest of the JavaScript.

If you `yarn deploy` our application and navigate to the **Network** tab in DevTools, you'll see something similar to the following:

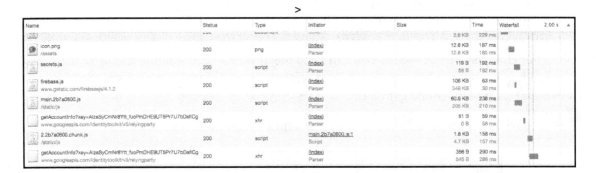

We load our main file and then whatever chunk is relevant to the current URL, but then we stop.

We're not loading the other routes during the idle time of our application! We need some way to trigger that loading process as soon as the initial route rendering is done, as soon as the `App` has mounted.

I think you know where this is going. In the `componentDidMount` method of `App`, we simply need to call our three loading methods:

```
componentDidMount() {
    this.notifications = new NotificationResource(
        firebase.messaging(),
        firebase.database()
    );
    firebase.auth().onAuthStateChanged(user => {
        if (user) {
            this.setState({ user });
            this.listenForMessages();
            this.notifications.changeUser(user);
        } else {
            this.props.history.push('/login');
        }
    });
    this.listenForMessages();
    this.listenForInstallBanner();
    loadChat();
    loadLogin();
    loadUser();
}
```

Now, whenever we're done rendering the current route, we'll get the other routes ready to go as well.

If you open the **Performance** tab of DevTools again, you will see this reflected in the network requests:

To the left, the bottom yellow chunk is our `main.js` file being loaded. This means our app can start initialized. To the right, the three yellow blocks correspond to our three route chunks. The one we need is loaded first, followed soon after by the other two.

We're now using much more of our application's idle time, spreading out the work of initializing our app.

# Summary

We covered a lot in this chapter, taking enormous strides to a more performative app. We split up our JavaScript by route and streamlined the loading process so that we load what we need and defer the rest to idle time.

However, all of this was really just paving the way for the next section. We need our app to perform under all network conditions, even an absence of any network. How can we make our application work offline?

Next, we dive into the world of caching and further improve our app's performance for any network condition, even the absence of a network.

# 12
# Ready to Cache

We've made enormous strides in the performance of our application. Our JavaScript is now split into smaller chunks based on the routes of our application, and we've deferred loading the less important bits until our app has some idle time. We've also introduced progressive enhancement to show our users content as soon as possible, and learned a lot about how to analyze our app's performance according to RAIL metrics.

However, there remains one central, core inefficiency in our web application. If our user leaves our page to go elsewhere (I know, how dare they) and then returns, we repeat the same process all over again: download the `index.html`, download the different JavaScript bundles, download the images, and so on.

We're asking our user to download the exact same files, over and over and over, every time they visit the page. Their device has more than enough memory to store those files for us. Why don't we just save them to the user's device, and then retrieve them as needed?

Welcome to caching. In this chapter, we'll cover these things:

- What is caching?
- The Cache API
- Using the Cache API in our service worker
- Testing our caching

# What is caching?

**Caching** is the act of reducing network requests or computation. Backend caching may consist of saving the result of a rigorous computation (say, generating statistics) so that when the client requests it a second time, we don't have to crunch the numbers again. Client-side caching usually consists of saving the response of a network request so that we don't have to make that call again.

As we said before, **service workers** are bits of code that sit between our application and the network. This means they are perfect for caching, as they can intercept a network request and respond with the requested file, grabbing it from the cache instead of the server; time is saved.

From a broader perspective, you can think of caching as not having to do the same thing more than once, using memory to store the result.

The upside of caching with Progressive Web Apps is that since the cache is stored in device memory, it's available regardless of network connectivity. This means everything stored in the cache can be accessed whether or not the device is connected. All of a sudden, our website is available offline.

For mobile users skipping between Wi-Fi zones, the convenience factor can be huge, giving them the ability to quickly check a message from a friend or a set of directions (anyone who has ever traveled without a roaming plan will know this feeling). Neither is this solely an advantage for purely offline users; for users with intermittent or low-quality connections, being able to continue working without a loss of functionality as the network skips in and out is a big win.

So, with one fell stroke, we can improve our app's performance for all our users and make it available offline. However, before we get to work implementing caching in Chatastrophe (hopefully, not a cachetastrophe), let's look at a story about the importance of caching.

# The importance of caching

In 2013, the US government launched `https://healthcare.gov/`, a website for citizens to sign up for the Affordable Care Act (also known as **Obamacare**). From the get-go, the site was plagued with serious technological problems. For thousands of people, it simply wouldn't load.

To be fair, the site was under enormous strain, visited an estimated 20 million times in its first month of operation (source--`http://www.bbc.com/news/world-us-canada-24613022`), but that strain was to be expected.

If you were building a website for millions of people to sign up for health care (all starting at the same time), performance would probably be at the top of your mind, but in the end, `https://healthcare.gov/` failed to deliver.

In response to the crisis (which threatened the credibility of the ACA), the administration put together a team to fix the problems, kind of like the Avengers, but software developers (so not the Avengers at all).

Given the goal of the site, the engineers were shocked to find that `https://healthcare.gov/` implemented no basic caching. None. So every time a user visited the site, the server had to deal with a network request and generate the information to reply.

This lack of caching had a compounding effect. The first wave of users clogged up the pipes, so the second wave of users got a loading screen. In response, they refreshed their screen, making more and more network requests, and so on.

Once the Devengers implemented caching, they cut the response time down by three-fourths. From then on, the site was able to handle even peak traffic.

Chatastrophe may not be dealing with `https://healthcare.gov/` levels of traffic (yet...), but caching is always a good idea.

# The Cache API

The mechanism we will use for caching is the **Web Cache API**.

> Note that the Mozilla Developer Network defines the Cache API as **experimental technology**, and as of August 2017, it only has the support of Chrome, Firefox, and the latest version of Opera.

The API specification has a few quirks we need to talk about. First, you can store multiple cache objects in the cache. In this way, we're able to store multiple versions of our cache, named whatever string we like.

That said, the browser has a limit of how much data it can store from any one site. If the cache gets too full, it may simply delete all data from that origin, so our best bet is to store the bare minimum.

However, there's an additional difficulty. Items in the cache never expire, unless explicitly deleted, so if we keep trying to stuff new cache objects into our cache, eventually it'll get too full and delete everything. Managing, updating, and deleting cache objects is entirely up to us. We have to clean up our own mess, in other words.

# Methods

We will use five methods to interact with the Cache API: `open`, `addAll`, `match`, `keys`, and `delete`. In the following, **Caches** will refer to the Cache API itself, and **Cache** to a specific cache object, to distinguish between methods called on an individual cache versus the API itself:

- `Caches.open()` takes a cache object name (also known as a cache key) as an argument (it can be any string), and either creates a new cache object or opens an existing one by the same name. It returns a `Promise` that resolves with the cache object as a parameter, which we can then use.
- `Cache.addAll()` takes in an array of URLs. It'll then go fetch those URLs from the server, and store the resulting file in the current cache object. Its little cousin is `Cache.add`, which does the same with a single URL.
- `Caches.match()` takes a network request as an argument (we'll see how to grab that as we go ahead). It looks in the cache for a file that matches the URL, and returns a `Promise` that resolves with that file. We can then return that file, superseding the need to make the request to the server. Its big brother is `Caches.matchAll()`.
- `Caches.keys()` returns the names of all the existing cache objects. We can then delete the outdated ones by passing their key to `Caches.delete()`.

The last method in the Cache API, which we won't use here but which may be of interest, is `Caches.put`. This takes a network request and fetches it, and then saves the result to the cache. This is useful if you want to cache every request without having to define what the URLs are ahead of time.

# The asset manifest

Our build process automatically generates an `asset-manifest.json` file for us, with a list of every JavaScript file our application contains. It looks something like this:

```
{
    "main.js": "static/js/main.8d0d0660.js",
    "static/js/0.8d0d0660.chunk.js": "static/js/0.8d0d0660.chunk.js",
    "static/js/1.8d0d0660.chunk.js": "static/js/1.8d0d0660.chunk.js",
    "static/js/2.8d0d0660.chunk.js": "static/js/2.8d0d0660.chunk.js"
}
```

In other words, we have a list of every JS file we want to cache. More importantly, the asset manifest is updated with the new hash of every file, so we don't have to worry about keeping that up to date.

We can thus use the URLs in the asset manifest alongside the `Cache.addAll()` method to instantly cache all our JavaScript assets in one go. We'll also need to manually add our static assets (images) to the cache, but to do so, we'll have to tap into our service worker life cycle methods and do some basic setup.

# Setting up our cache

In this section, we'll move through our three main service worker life cycle events, and interact with our cache individually in each event. By the end, we will have automatic caching for all static files.

A warning, though--working with caches in development is, at best, tolerable, and at worst, infuriating. "Why aren't you updating?" we yell at our screen, until we realize that our cache has been serving up old code; it happens to the best of us. In this section, we'll take steps to avoid caching our development files and dodge this bullet, but in the future, remember that weird errors are probably caused by caching.

> *There are only two hard things in Computer Science: cache invalidation and naming things.*
>
> *-- Phil Karlton*

And another take:

> *There are two hard problems in computer science: cache invalidation, naming things, and off-by-1 errors.*

*-- Leon Bambrick*

# The install event

When our service worker installs, we want to go ahead and set up our cache, and begin caching the relevant assets. So, our step-by-step guide to our install event goes like this:

1. Open up the relevant cache.
2. Get our asset manifest.
3. Parse the JSON.
4. Add the relevant URLs to our cache, plus our static assets.

Let's open up `firebase-messaging-sw.js` and get to work!

If you still have the `console.log` event listener for install, great! Delete the `console.log`; otherwise, set it up as follows:

```
self.addEventListener('install', function() {

});
```

Right above this function, we'll also assign our cache object name to a variable:

```
const CACHE_NAME = 'v1';
```

This name can be literally anything, but we'll want to up the version every time we deploy, just to ensure that old caches are invalidated and everyone gets the freshest possible code.

Now, let's run through our checklist.

# Opening up the cache

Before we get to the good stuff, we need to talk about extendable events.

Once our service worker is activated and installed, it may immediately go into "waiting" mode--waiting for an event to occur to which it must respond. However, we don't want it to go into waiting mode while we're in the middle of opening the cache, which is an asynchronous operation. So, we need a way of telling our service worker, "Hey, don't consider yourself fully installed until the cache is populated."

The way we do so is via `event.waitUntil()`. This method extends the life of an event (here, the install event) until all Promises within it are resolved.

It looks as shown:

```
self.addEventListener('install', event => {
 event.waitUntil(
   // Promise goes here
 );
});
```

Now we can open our cache. Our Cache API is available in the caches global variable, so we can just call `caches.open()`:

```
const CACHE_NAME = 'v1';
self.addEventListener('install', event => {
 event.waitUntil(
   caches.open(CACHE_NAME)
     .then(cache => {
       });
 );
});
```

Since no cache object with the name `'v1'` will currently exist, we will automatically create one. Once we get that cache object, we can move to step 2.

# Fetching the asset manifest

Fetching the asset manifest sounds exactly like it sounds:

```
self.addEventListener('install', event => {
 event.waitUntil(
   caches.open(CACHE_NAME)
     .then(cache => {
       fetch('asset-manifest.json')
         .then(response => {
```

```
              if (response.ok) {
                }
              })
          });
      );
    });
```

Note that we should have no asset-manifest in development; we need to ensure that the request response is okay before proceeding, lest we throw an error.

## Parsing the JSON

Our `asset-manifest.json` returns, rather surprisingly, some JSON. Let's parse it:

```
self.addEventListener('install', event => {
  event.waitUntil(
    caches.open(CACHE_NAME)
      .then(cache => {
        fetch('asset-manifest.json')
          .then(response => {
            if (response.ok) {
              response.json().then(manifest => {

              });
            }
          })
      });
    );
  });
```

Now we have a manifest variable that is a plain JavaScript object matching the content of `asset-manifest.json`.

## Adding the relevant URLs to the cache

Since we have a JavaScript object to access the URLs, we can pick and choose what we want to cache, but in this case, we want everything, so let's iterate over the object and get an array of URLs:

```
response.json().then(manifest => {
  const urls = Object.keys(manifest).map(key => manifest[key]);
})
```

We also want to cache the `index.html` and our icon, so let's push in `/` and
`/assets/icon.png`:

```
response.json().then(manifest => {
  const urls = Object.keys(manifest).map(key => manifest[key]);
  urls.push('/');
  urls.push('/assets/icon.png');
})
```

Now, we can add all these URLs to the cache with `cache.addAll()`. Note that we're
referring to the specific cache object we opened, and not the general caches variable:

```
self.addEventListener('install', event => {
  event.waitUntil(
    caches.open(CACHE_NAME).then(cache => {
      fetch('asset-manifest.json').then(response => {
        if (response.ok) {
          response.json().then(manifest => {
            const urls = Object.keys(manifest).map(key => manifest[key]);
            urls.push('/');
            urls.push('/assets/icon.png');
            cache.addAll(urls);
          });
        }
      });
    })
  );
});
```

Done! We have caching, but it's not worth much yet, as we have no way of retrieving items
from the cache. Let's do that next.

# The fetch event

When our application requests a file from the server, we want to intercept that request
inside our service worker, and respond with the cached file (if it exists).

We can do so by listening to the fetch event, as illustrated:

```
self.addEventListener('fetch', event => {

});
```

The event passed in as argument has two properties of interest. The first is
`event.request`, which is the target URL. We'll use that to see whether we have the item in
our cache, but the event also has a method called `respondWith`, which basically means
"stop this network request from going through, and respond to it with the following."

Here's the unintuitive part--we're essentially canceling this fetch event as soon as we call
`event.respondWith`. This means if we don't have the item in our cache, we have to start
another fetch request (which does not, thankfully, trigger another event listener; no
recursion here). This is something to keep in mind.

So, let's call `event.respondWith`, and then use `caches.match` to see whether we have a
file matching the URL:

```
self.addEventListener('fetch', event => {
  event.respondWith(
    caches.match(event.request).then(response => {

    });
  );
});
```

The response, in this case, will be either the file in question or null. If it's the file, we return
it; otherwise, we make another fetch request and return its result. Here's the one-line
version:

```
self.addEventListener('fetch', event => {
  event.respondWith(
    caches.match(event.request).then(response => {
      return response || fetch(event.request);
    })
  );
});
```

That's it! Now all fetch requests for files in our asset manifest will go to the cache first, and
only make an actual network request if the said file isn't there.

# The activate event

The activate event is the first of our three service worker events to take place, so it may
seem odd that we're talking about it last, but there's a good reason.

The activate event is when we do cache clean up. We ensure that we get rid of any expired
cache objects so that our share of the browser cache doesn't get too cluttered and become
terminated.

To do so, we basically delete any cache object whose name doesn't match the current value of CACHE_NAME.

"But Scott," you say, "what if our service worker doesn't update properly, and still contains the old CACHE_NAME?" This is a valid point. However, as said, our service worker should automatically update whenever there is a byte-sized difference between it and the previous service worker, so that should not be a concern.

Our process is less intensive this time, but let's still break it down:

1. Grab the list of cache names.
2. Loop over them.
3. Delete any cache whose key doesn't match CACHE_NAME.

A quick reminder--you can have multiple caches if you want to keep your CSS in a seperate cache from your JS. There's no real benefit of doing so, but you may like things organized. An approach that will work is to create a CACHE_NAMES object instead, as follows:

```
const VERSION = 'v1'
const CACHE_NAMES = {
  css: `css-${VERSION}`,
  js: `js-${VERSION}`
};
```

Then, in the subsequent steps, we'll have to iterate over that object; just something to keep in mind.

Okay, let's get to work.

# Grab the list of cache names

Again, we have to do an event.waitUntil() while we complete this async code. This means we'll have to eventually return a Promise to the event.waitUntil(), which will affect how we write our code.

First, we grab the list of cache keys, by calling cache.keys(), which returns a promise:

```
self.addEventListener('activate', event => {
  event.waitUntil(
    cache.keys().then(keyList => {

    })
  );
});
```

# Loop over them

We need to go through each key and call `caches.delete()` if it doesn't match our `CACHE_NAME`. Since we may have multiple caches to delete, and multiple calls to `caches.delete()`, which returns a `Promise` in itself, we'll map over `keyList` and return a set of Promises using `Promise.all()`.

Here's what it looks like:

```
self.addEventListener('activate', event => {
  event.waitUntil(
    caches.keys().then(keyList => {
      Promise.all(keyList.map(key => {

      }));
    })
  );
});
```

Delete any cache whose key doesn't match `CACHE_NAME`.

A simple `if` statement, and a call to `caches.delete()`, and we're done:

```
self.addEventListener('activate', event => {
  event.waitUntil(
    caches.keys().then(keyList => {
      Promise.all(
        keyList.map(key => {
          if (key !== CACHE_NAME) {
            return caches.delete(key);
          }
        })
      );
    })
  );
});
```

Now our caches will be exactly the size we want them to be (only on cache object) and will be checked every time our service worker activates.

There is, thus, an inherent mechanism to how our cache stays up to date. Every time we update our JavaScript, we should update the version in our service worker. This causes our service worker to update, and thus reactivate, which triggers a check and invalidation of the previous caches; a beautiful system.

# Testing our cache

Run your app locally quickly with `yarn start` to check for any obvious errors (typos and such), and if all looks good, fire up `yarn deploy`.

Open your live application and the Chrome DevTools. Turn off **Update on reload** under **Application** | **Service Workers**, refresh once, and then go to the **Network** tab. You should see something like the following:

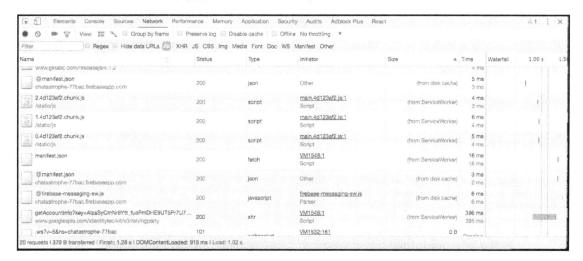

 If this doesn't work, try Unregistering any service workers under **Application** | **Service Workers**, and then reload twice.

The key point is (from service worker) beside our JavaScript files. Our static assets are being served up by our service worker cache, and if you scroll to the top of the network tab, you'll see this:

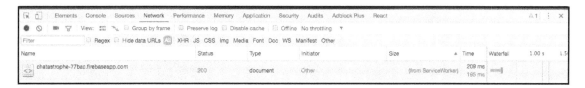

The document itself is being served from the service worker, which means we can run our app under any network condition, even offline; let's try it. Click on the **Offline** checkbox at the top of the **Network** tab, and click on reload.

If all goes well, there should be no difference between our application's load time, even though we have no network connection! Our application still loads, and so do our chat messages.

The message loading is a benefit of the database of Firebase, not really our doing, but having the document itself load from the cache, that's the real achievement!

Of course, our UX isn't set up well for offline access. We should have some way of informing the user they're currently offline, perhaps with some sort of dialog, but we'll leave that as a stretch goal.

# Summary

We achieved the progressive dream--an application that works under any network conditions, including an absence of any network at all. Caching is a difficult subject, so give yourself a pat on the back for making it this far.

However, before we get too excited and submit our prototype to the Chatastrophe board, let's ensure that we did things right. We need some way to put a rubber stamp on our project, which says, "Approved! This is a Progressive Web App!".

Luckily, a little startup by the name of Google has given us a tool to do exactly like that.

Up next is auditing our completed progressive web app, AKA the victory lap.

# 13
# Auditing Our App

**Auditing** is a way of confirming that our Progressive Web App is a true PWA, that it lives up to the standards of the name. This audit is an important last step for us to check our work and ensure that our app is as good as it can be in terms of PWA functionality.

As mentioned previously, the biggest champion of Progressive Web Apps is Google. Not only are their Chrome browser and Android operating systems the most PWA-friendly of all, Google puts a great deal of effort into educating developers on how and why to build a PWA. As you move forward (beyond this book) into the world of the PWA, you'll probably often turn to their documentation.

However, Google provides another way to light the way forward to the progressive web. To ensure the quality of your web page or application, they have released a set of tools to measure your site against a set criteria. The main tool they use to do so is called Lighthouse.

Here's what we'll cover in this chapter:

- What is Lighthouse?
- What criteria does it follow?
- What is the Audits tab in DevTools?
- Running our first audit
- Evaluating the readout
- Using the Lighthouse CLI

# What is Lighthouse?

In a sentence, **Lighthouse** is a tool that runs your site and tells you how progressive it really is, based on a set of specific criteria.

It does so by trying to load the page under a variety of conditions (including a 3G network and offline) and assessing how the page responds. It also checks for some PWA standbys, such as a splash screen and a service worker.

# The criteria

The following criteria are essentially a checklist that Lighthouse follows while looking at your app. Each "test" is a simple yes/no. If you pass all the tests, you get a score of 100. That's what we want!

Here's a written list of the criteria, as of August 2017:

- **Registers a Service Worker**: The service worker is the technology that enables your app to use many Progressive Web App features, such as offline, add to homescreen, and push notifications.
- **Responds with a 200 when offline:** If you're building a Progressive Web App, consider using a service worker so that your app can work offline.
- **Contains some content when JavaScript is not available**: Your app should display some content when JavaScript is disabled, even if it's just a warning to the user that JavaScript is required to use the app.
- **Configured for a custom splash screen:** A default splash screen will be constructed for your app, but satisfying these requirements guarantees a high-quality splash screen that transitions the user from tapping on the home screen icon to your app's first paint.
- **Uses HTTPS**: All sites should be protected with HTTPS, even ones that don't handle sensitive data. HTTPS prevents intruders from tampering with or passively listening in on the communications between your app and your users, and is a prerequisite for HTTP/2 and many new web platform APIs.
- **Redirects HTTP traffic to HTTPS**: If you've already set up HTTPS, ensure that you redirect all HTTP traffic to HTTPS.
- **Page load is fast enough on 3G:** This criterion is satisfied if the **Time To Interactive** duration is shorter than 10 seconds, as defined by the PWA Baseline Checklist (source--`https://developers.google.com/web/progressive-web-apps/checklist`). Network throttling is required (specifically, RTT latencies >= 150 RTT are expected).

- **User can be prompted to install the Web App:** While users can manually add your site to their home screen, the prompt (also known as app install banner) will proactively prompt the user to install the app if the various requirements are met and the user has moderate engagement with your site.
- **Address bar matches brand colors:** The browser address bar can be themed to match your site. A `theme-color` meta tag will upgrade the address bar when a user browses the site, and the manifest theme color will apply the same theme site-wide once it's been added to the home screen.
- **Has a <meta name="viewport"> tag with width or initial-scale:** Add a `viewport` meta tag to optimize your app for mobile screens.
- **Content is sized correctly for the viewport:** If the width of your app's content doesn't match the width of the viewport, your app might not be optimized for mobile screens.

# The Audits tab

Until the release of Chrome 60, Lighthouse was only available in beta version as a Chrome extension or command-line tool. Now, however, it has its very own place in the Chrome DevTools, in the new **Audits tab**.

Included in the **Audits** tab, alongside the Lighthouse PWA audit, is a selection of other benchmark tests, including performance and web best practices. We'll focus on the PWA test and performance tests, but feel free to run the other tests as well.

Another useful feature of the Audits tab is the ability to save previous audits, to get a sort of history of your application as you improve it.

Okay, enough talk. Let's go ahead and run our first audit!

# Our first audit

Open up your DevTools, navigate to the **Audits** tab, and click on **Run Audit**.

It should take a few seconds, and then give you a nice summary of how our site looks, drumroll. How good is our Progressive Web App?:

Not bad at all. In fact, it doesn't get better than that in the PWA category. Give yourself a pat on the back and perhaps a high-five for a job well-done. Let's evaluate the readout, and then decide whether we want to move on or aim for 100% in all categories.

Please note that since Lighthouse is under active development, your scores may not match the above due to new criteria. In that case, I encourage you to take a look at what Lighthouse is complaining about, and see if you can solve it to get to that '100' score.

# Evaluating the readout

If your results don't match the preceding, there are two possibilities:

- Chrome has added a new test that our app does not fulfill. As we've mentioned many times, PWAs are an evolving technology, so this is certainly possible.
- You missed some step in the book; happens to the best of us.

In either case, I encourage you to investigate and try to solve the root issue. Google provides documentation for every test criteria, which is a good place to start.

In our case, the only test we didn't pass with flying colors was Performance. Let's look at the reason we didn't:

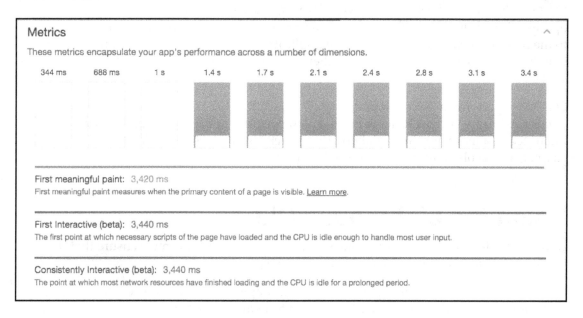

As we see here, our first meaningful paint takes about three seconds. Note that our app shell is not considered a meaningful paint, though it does improve the perceived performance of the page. Chrome is smart enough to know that it is not until our login form or chat container appears that we actually have meaningful content on the screen-- stuff the user can actually use.

The reason it takes over three seconds to display that meaningful content, though, is that we need to wait for our JavaScript to load, boot up, and then load whether our user is currently logged in, and then either load the chat messages or redirect to login. That's a lot of subsequent steps.

Is this a solvable problem? Perhaps. We can wire up some way of finding out whether our user is logged in before React loads (in other words, move some JavaScript out of our main app). We can move both the chat container and the login form out of React to ensure that they can be rendered before the library loads, and then come up with some means of replacing them once React initializes (the challenge being replacing inputs without erasing anything the user has started typing).

All the mentioned challenges fall under the category of optimizing the critical render path. For anyone who wants to dive deeper into performance optimization, I encourage you to try it out. From a business perspective, however, that's a lot of (potentially buggy) optimization for little gain. Our users already receive content in around 400 ms, according to the previous benchmarks, and the full application in just over three seconds. Remember that, thanks to caching, most users will then get a much faster load time in their subsequent visits.

Our lower performance score demonstrates, in fact, the cost-benefit of using a weighty JavaScript library such as React to build a high performance application. For those interested in a more lightweight alternative, check out the section on Preact in the next chapter, a possible solution to the preceding problem.

# Using the Lighthouse CLI

Running the tests from the **Audits** tab is nice and easy, but how can we ensure that the quality of our application is maintained before we push it live?

The answer is to incorporate Lighthouse into our deploy process, and use it to assess our build automatically. This is similar to having a test suite run when we hit `yarn deploy`. Fortunately, Google supplies with a Lighthouse CLI for exactly this purpose.

Let's install it with the following:

```
yarn add --dev lighthouse
```

Here, our goal is to run Lighthouse on our application whenever we run `yarn deploy`. To do so, we have to make a custom deploy script.

If you open up our `package.json`, you'll see the following under `scripts`:

```
"scripts": {
  "build": "node_modules/.bin/webpack --config webpack.config.prod.js",
  "start": "node_modules/.bin/webpack-dev-server",
  "deploy": "npm run build && firebase deploy"
},
```

Let's change that to the following:

```
"scripts": {
  "build": "node_modules/.bin/webpack --config webpack.config.prod.js",
  "start": "node_modules/.bin/webpack-dev-server",
  "deploy": "npm run build && node scripts/assess.js && firebase deploy"
},
```

We will use node to run a custom build script written in JavaScript. Create `scripts/` folder in your directory root, along with the `assess.js` file.

Our process will be as follows:

1. Serve our `build` folder locally, so it runs in the browser.
2. Use Lighthouse to assess the served page.
3. Console log the results.

Let's add the package we need to serve our `build` folder:

```
yarn add --dev serve
```

Note that we're saving this and `lighthouse` as `dev` dependencies, given that we'll never use them in production.

# Serving our build folder

Inside our new `scripts/assess.js`, require the `serve` package:

```
const serve = require('serve');
```

All we want to do is `serve` our newly compiled `build` folder on `port:5000`, which looks like this:

```
const server = serve('./build', {
 port: 5000
});
```

We can stop the server at any time by running `server.stop()`. We'll do that once our scores are displayed.

# Using Lighthouse to assess the served page

Now, let's require two more tools at the top of `assess.js`:

```
const lighthouse = require('lighthouse');
const chromeLauncher = require('lighthouse/chrome-launcher');
```

`chromeLauncher` will allow us to open up Chrome to the target page, and then run Lighthouse. Let's make a function called `launchChromeAndRunLighthouse` to do exactly this:

```
function launchChromeAndRunLighthouse(url, flags= {}, config = null) {

}
```

We can optionally pass in some flags and config, which we won't use here (flags can be used to turn on logging as the process unfolds).

Inside the function, we'll launch Chrome, set the port for Lighthouse to run on, and then run it. Lastly, we'll stop Chrome:

```
function launchChromeAndRunLighthouse(url, flags = {}, config = null) {
  return chromeLauncher.launch().then(chrome => {
    flags.port = chrome.port;
    return lighthouse(url, flags, config).then(results =>
      chrome.kill().then(() => results));
  });
}
```

This function is taken directly from the Lighthouse CLI documentation, by the way.

Okay, now for the last step. We'll run our function with our chosen URL (put this at the bottom of the file, below the `serve` command):

```
launchChromeAndRunLighthouse('http://localhost:5000', {}).then(results => {
  server.stop();
});
```

Once we have our results, we stop the server, but we need to display our results properly.

# Logging the results

The results variable comes in as an object. It gives a detailed breakdown of each category with the score given, but we only care about trouble areas. Above our function invocation, let's add a score cutoff:

```
const CUTOFF = 90
launchChromeAndRunLighthouse('http://localhost:5000', {}).then(results => {
```

We'll use this to say "only show results that score less than 90/100."

The process of logging out the results isn't too exciting, so we won't walk through it here in depth. Here's the complete file:

```
const serve = require('serve');
const lighthouse = require('lighthouse');
const chromeLauncher = require('lighthouse/chrome-launcher');

function launchChromeAndRunLighthouse(url, flags = {}, config = null) {
 return chromeLauncher.launch().then(chrome => {
   flags.port = chrome.port;
   return lighthouse(url, flags, config).then(results =>
     chrome.kill().then(() => results));
 });
}

const server = serve('./build', {
 port: 5000
})

const CUTOFF = 90

launchChromeAndRunLighthouse('http://localhost:5000', {}).then(results => {
 score = results.score
 const catResults = results.reportCategories.map(cat => {
   if (cat.score < CUTOFF) {
     cat.audits.forEach(audit => {
       if (audit.score < CUTOFF) {
         const result = audit.result
         if (result.score) {
           console.warn(result.description + ': ' + result.score)
         } else {
           console.warn(result.description)
         }
         if (results.displayValue) {
           console.log('Value: ' + result.displayValue)
         }
         console.log(result.helpText)
         console.log(' ')
       }
     })
   }
   return cat
 })
 catResults.forEach(cat => {
   console.log(cat.name, cat.score)
 })
 server.stop()
});
```

If you run `node scripts/assess.js` from your Terminal, you should see a list of problem areas as well as a final score for each category. Bring it all together by running `yarn deploy`, and you'll see those scores appear before the Firebase deployment.

Now we have an easy and clean way to keep up to date on the status of our application as it evolves, without having to launch the site ourselves to test it.

# Summary

Done! We fully audited our application, and it passed with flying colors in every category. We have a working Progressive Web Application. In this chapter, we learned what Lighthouse was, and why it's important to verify our PWA. We also added it as part of our deployment process to ensure that our app continues to meet the quality standards. We can now consider our app complete in every aspect.

Next, we'll talk about the subsequent steps as well as useful resources for growing your knowledge of PWAs, but first, about submitting our app to your friend and the Chatastrophe board.

# 14
# Conclusion and Next Steps

"... and this is how the app scores according to Google. As you can see, it hits every criteria for a Progressive Web App, which will fit well with our business goal of a global—"

"Yeah, yeah," your friend says, waving his hand. "Very cool. Great. Good job. But what about the pivot?"

"What?" you ask.

"Didn't you get the memo? I sent out a memo to your company email a month ago."

"I didn't know I had a company email."

"Oh." Your friend frowns. "I thought you were good with technology."

"But I didn't know-"

"No matter. I can summarize. The company has pivoted. Chat is great and all, but what if we took it one step further? What if we made it a social network? Picture it--the sharability of Facebook with the video streaming of Netflix with the ridesharing of Uber, all in one, on the blockchain..."

Your friend continues to talk as you head for the door.

# Next steps

We've covered every step it takes to make a React application into a PWA but, as always, there's more to learn.

This concluding chapter is divided into four sections. First, we'll go over a list of useful resources to continue your PWA journey. Then, we'll cover important libraries that will help automate certain aspects of PWA development, or take your app to the next level. Third, I'll list some of my favorite articles of developing Progressive Web Apps. As a last note, we'll take a look at some possible stretch goals for you to expand and improve on Chatastrophe, if you accept the challenge.

Many of the following resources were discovered through two excellent repositiories: **awesome-pwa** (`https://github.com/hemanth/awesome-pwa` ) by GitHub user *Hemanth*, and **awesome-progressive-web-apps** (`https://github.com/TalAter/awesome-progressive-web-apps` ) by *TalAter*.

We'll look at the following:

- Learning resources to expand your knowledge
- Case studies of successful PWAs
- Example apps to get inspiration from
- Must-read articles about the rise of PWAs
- Tools you can use to make building future PWAs easier
- Stretch goals for Chatastrophe

# Learning resources

Learning resources are as follows:

- **Progressive Web Apps Documentation**: Google's official documentation on Progressive Web Apps. This should be your first stop to brush on concepts or read about best practices. It also provides a summary of the benefits of PWAs and links to tools such as Lighthouse.

    `https://developers.google.com/web/progressive-web-apps/`

- **Your First Progressive Web App**: A step-by-step tutorial for building your first Progressive Web App, or in your case, your second one. If you want to see what building a PWA without React will look like, check out this tutorial. This is nice and in depth and covers each concept thoroughly.

  ```
  https://developers.google.com/web/fundamentals/getting-started/
  codelabs/your-first-pwapp
  ```

- **Offline Web Applications**: A free course created by Google and hosted by Udacity, on offline-first web applications. The content is divided into three parts: Why Offline First, Service Workers, and Caching. Some parts, such as the service worker section, will likely be review, but this course also dives into IndexedDB for local storage.

  ```
  https://www.udacity.com/course/offline-web-applications--ud899
  ```

- **Service Worker Primer**: Google's introduction to Service Workers. Much of the code will look familiar from the service worker section on this book, but it is a handy resource nonetheless. Matt Gaunt does a great job of explaining the basics.

  ```
  https://developers.google.com/web/fundamentals/getting-started/
  primers/service-workers
  ```

- **Service Worker 101**: A more colorful guide to service workers, this lovely resource contains a series of diagrams to take you through the service worker life cycle and more. Print this out and stick it on your desk if you're unsure about service workers.

  ```
  https://github.com/delapuente/service-workers-101
  ```

- **Getting Started with Progressive Web Apps**: A blog post by *Addy Osmani*, on the Chrome development team (we'll see him a lot in this resource section). This is a great high-level introduction to the benefits of PWA and also introduces some boilerplates to get started.

  ```
  https://addyosmani.com/blog/getting-started-with-progressive-web-
  apps/
  ```

- **Using the Push API**: The Mozilla Developer Network guide to the Push API. If you want to use push notifications in your PWA without relying on Firebase Cloud Notifications, start here.

  ```
  https://developer.mozilla.org/en-US/docs/Web/API/Push_API/Using_
  the_Push_API
  ```

- **Using the Cache API**: The Mozilla Developer Network guide to the Cache API. Not much new here that we didn't cover in the chapter on caching, but it's good to refer back to, given the Cache API's "experimental" status. The technology can evolve from its current status, so keep this as a reference.

  ```
  https://developer.mozilla.org/en-US/docs/Web/API/Cache
  ```

- **Increasing Engagement with App Install Banners**: The how and why of app install banners. A thorough FAQ answers any questions you may have. There's also a great tutorial on deferring the prompt, which you can use to cement the concepts we covered in our Chapter 9, *Making Our App Installable with a Manifest*.

  ```
  https://developers.google.com/web/updates/2015/03/increasing-
  engagement-with-app-install-banners-in-chrome-for-android?hl=en
  ```

- **Web Fundamentals- Performance**: Google's resources on building performative web applications. It should be noted that Google has a specific philosophy for performance that falls into a PWA model, but is not necessarily the only route to better performance. That said, a great (if at times overly technical) resource for anyone interested in speed (which you should be!).

  ```
  https://developers.google.com/web/fundamentals/performance/
  ```

- **Introducing RAIL: A User-Centric Model For Performance**: This article opens with "There's no shortage of performance advice, is there?". True words, though the advice of *Paul Irish* and *Paul Lewis* is better than most. This article introduces RAIL with special attention to why we should follow this metric. The answer? The user should come first.

  ```
  https://www.smashingmagazine.com/2015/10/rail-user-centric-model-
  performance/
  ```

- **The Progressive Web App Newsletter**: My free newsletter to keep you up to date on the world of PWAs, with tutorials, articles, interesting projects, and more. If you ever want to get in touch, just click on "Reply" on the next issue. I would love to hear from you.

  ```
  http://pwa-newsletter.com/
  ```

- **Website Performance Optimization**: Another Google and Udacity course, this time on optimizing performance. It gives an introduction to DevTools and dives into concepts such as the critical rendering path. This course should take you about a week to get through.

  ```
  https://www.udacity.com/course/website-performance-optimization--
  ud884
  ```

- **Browser Rendering Optimization**: Here's another one! This course is subtitled "Building 60 FPS Web Apps", which (as our RAIL metric advises) is a worthy goal. It can be considered a more in-depth version of the preceding course. After this one, you can call yourself a web performance expert.

  ```
  https://www.udacity.com/course/browser-rendering-optimization--
  ud860
  ```

- **Progressive Web Apps with React**: *Addy Osmani* at it again. Here, he takes us through building a PWA with React. Note that this tutorial is more an overview than a step-by-step guide, but it was an invaluable resource to me in writing this book. He also provides many links to additional articles and resources to expand your knowledge even further.

  ```
  >https://medium.com/@addyosmani/progressive-web-apps-with-react-
  js-part-i-introduction-50679aef2b12
  ```

- **Service Worker Cookbook**: Everything you could ever want to know about service workers. Seriously, this is an amazing resource that will make you an expert before you know it. If you are excited about this new technology and want to dive deeper, here's your chance.

  ```
  https://serviceworke.rs/
  ```

- **Retrofit Your Website as a PWA**: Most companies won't be looking at building a PWA from scratch anytime soon. Instead, they'll want to add PWA features to their existing site or app. Here's a great starter guide for doing so, with plenty of screenshots.

  ```
  https://www.sitepoint.com/retrofit-your-website-as-a-progressive-
  web-app/
  ```

# Case studies

Do you need to convince a boss to try a Progressive Web Application? Check out the following case studies from big companies that embraced the PWA world (Chatastrophe Inc. removed from list following bankruptcy).

# Building the Google I/O 2016 Progressive Web App

The Google I/O 2016 app (nicknamed IOWA) was built with Firebase and Polymer. This is how they did it. A much more technical guide that introduces several advanced concepts; this is a great way to peek into a next-level PWA.

```
https://developers.google.com/web/showcase/2016/iowa2016
```

# AliExpress case study

AliExpress is the most visited e-commerce site in Russia. By switching to a PWA, they increased conversions from new users by 104%. They also increased time spent on the site by 74%. Those are big numbers, and make a compelling business case for PWAs.

```
https://developers.google.com/web/showcase/2016/aliexpress
```

# eXtra Electronics case study

How's this for a business improvement--100% more sales. That's what eXtra Electronics achieved from users arriving via web push notifications. In fact, web push notifications are now eXtra's biggest retention channel, beating out email. Push harder!

```
https://developers.google.com/web/showcase/2016/extra
```

# Jumia case study

Another hip hip hooray for web push notifications. Jumia increased conversions by 9X. They used to send an email to remind a customer about items left in their cart, but open rates were low. Enter notifications.

`https://developers.google.com/web/showcase/2016/jumia`

# Konga case study

Your users care about their data limits; don't make them suffer. Konga reduced data usage by 92%, comparing their native app to their PWA. In the end, users needed 84% less data to complete the first transaction. Consider the barrier for entry lowered.

`https://developers.google.com/web/showcase/2016/konga`

# SUUMO case study

With the addition of service workers and some other tweaks, the SUUMO team reduced load time by 75%. They also cashed in on the push notifications hype train, with a 31% open rate. The story behind the decision to try a PWA may sound familiar; the mobile experience was subpar, so the company pushed users toward the native app. Getting them to download the native app was a struggle, though, so they tried a PWA. Good learning--if your problem is retention, native apps are probably not the answer.

`https://developers.google.com/web/showcase/2016/suumo`

# Example applications

Want to see what a real live PWA looks like? Check out any of the following. A few also contain links to GitHub for you to view the source code.

# PWA.rocks

A collection of Progressive Web Apps and source for most of the following. If you ever need inspiration, make this your first stop. I also encourage you to add any PWAs you add to the list.

`https://pwa.rocks/`

# Flipboard

One of the biggest players in the PWA space, Flipboard's PWA is slim, fast, and beautiful. Flipboard has a full-featured native application, but also a PWA in order to hedge their bets in terms of user preference. If the content-heavy Flipboard can manage the performance guidelines of PWAs, the sky is the limit.

```
https://flipboard.com/
```

# React Hacker News

The ever-popular developer project: a clone of Hacker News, here using React. As an open source project, ReactHN is a great way to look into how to manage a complex frontend library with Progressive Web App fundamentals. Our good friend *Addy Osmani* is at work again. ReactHN is thus an inside look at how a Chrome developer will structure a PWA using a JavaScript-heavy library.

```
https://react-hn.appspot.com/
```

# Notes

A nice and slim example of a Progressive Web App, this one is worth looking at for beginners. You can find a link to the GitHub directly on the site and then poke around the structure of *Simon Evans* app. On the desktop, there's a clear distinction of the application shell from the content, which makes the concept particularly intuitive. Best of all, the app boasts a score of 94 on Lighthouse.

```
https://sii.im/playground/notes/
```

# Twitter

Perhaps you've heard of this one.

Twitter is the perfect example of a truly global application. Their application needs to be accessible by users on all continents, in all conditions (just look at the role Twitter played in organizing revolts in the Arab Spring).

To achieve global accessibility, the Twitter team managed to slim down their application to 1 MB and added all the PWA goodness discussed in this article: home screen installation, push notifications, and offline access.

```
https://lite.twitter.com/
```

## 2048 Puzzle

A PWA implementation by *Gabriele Cirulli* of the 2048 puzzle game originally created by Veewo Studio. It only works on mobile/touchscreen devices, but is an example of a game app being made into a PWA that is fast, efficient, and installable. Beware--for the uninitiated, the game is highly addictive.

The open source is available on GitHub, so you can take a look at the structure (particularly of the JavaScript, which requires ten files to make the game run). The dirty secret of this app, however, is that the creator never actually beat the game.

```
https://2048-opera-pwa.surge.sh/
```

# Articles to read

The following articles cover manifestos, tutorials, and lists, all about the rise of PWAs and the best ways to build them.

## Native apps are doomed

JavaScript guru *Eric Elliott* impassioned declaration in favor of Progressive Web Apps. It's a deep dive into the costs of native applications and the benefit of PWAs. It's good material to convince bosses and coworkers who are debating building for native. The follow-up article is also excellent.

```
https://medium.com/javascript-scene/native-apps-are-doomed-ac397148a2c0
```

## A BIG list of Progressive Web App tips & tricks

A grab bag of assorted PWA tips from *Dean Hume*. Check it out for fun stuff, such as offline Google Analytics and testing service workers (more on that as we go ahead).

```
https://deanhume.com/Home/BlogPost/a-big-list-of-progressive-web-app-tips-and-tricks/10160
```

## Testing service workers

Service workers are the heart and soul of Progressive Web App functionality. We want to ensure that they're working right. How can we unit test them?

`https://medium.com/dev-channel/testing-service-workers-318d7b016b19`

## Twitter Lite and High Performance React Progressive Web Apps at Scale

One of the Twitter Lite engineers dives into their build process, challenges, and gives recommendations after developing the PWA version of Twitter. As close to a how-to for deploying large-scale PWA's as you will get.

`https://medium.com/@paularmstrong/twitter-lite-and-high-performance-react-progressive-web-apps-at-scale-d28a00e780a3`

## Why are App Install Banners Still a thing?

An excellent summary of the cost of sticking to traditional apps when you're not a market leader and how Progressive Web Apps aim to solve this problem. Read to the end for some statistics from companies that switched from native apps to PWAs.

`https://medium.com/dev-channel/why-are-app-install-banners-still-a-thing-18f3952d349a`

## A Progressive Web Application with Vue JS

*Charles Bochet* combines VueJS, Webpack, and elements of Material Design to build a PWA. A great chance to try out PWA concepts in a new library.

`https://blog.sicara.com/a-progressive-web-application-with-vue-js-webpack-material-design-part-3-service-workers-offline-ed3184264fd1`

# Transforming an existing Angular application into a Progressive Web App

What does it take to transform a regular Angular app into a functional Progressive Web App? *Coskun Deniz* takes us through the steps, one by one.
https://medium.com/@cdeniz/transforming-an-existing-angular-application-into-a-progressive-web-app-d48869ba391f

# Progressing the Web

"Literally any website can, and should, be a progressive web app."

*Jeremy Keith* gives the main argument in his article as "Progressing the Web," and he's right. Making your app (or your static site) progressive is about offering an enhanced experienced for all your users. A good read for anyone tentative to jump into the world of PWAs.

https://medium.com/@adactio/progressing-the-web-9ab55f63f9fa

# Designed Degradations - UX Patterns for Hostile Environments

How a Chipotle restaurant can help improve your website. This article isn't about PWAs in particular, but fits right in with the idea of progressive enhancement, the concept that your website should work for everyone and then get better and better depending on their conditions (network speed, browser modernity, and so on).

https://uxdesign.cc/designed-degradations-ux-patterns-for-hostile-environments-7f308d819e50

# Instant Loading Web Apps With An Application Shell Architecture

An in-depth explanation of the app shell pattern. A must-read if you're in the development phase of a PWA.

https://medium.com/google-developers/instant-loading-web-apps-with-an-application-shell-architecture-7c0c2f10c73

# Trick users into thinking your site's faster than it is

A fantastic read that starts from the user's perspective (perceived time versus actual time) and moves into an explanation of the basic techniques you can leverage to decrease the perceived load time of your app.

```
http://www.creativebloq.com/features/trick-users-into-thinking-your-sites-
faster-than-it-is
```

# Apple's refusal to support Progressive Web Apps is a detriment to the future of the web

A refreshingly honest look at what it's like to develop a Progressive Web Application at this point in time and the struggles with iOS that come along with it. Read this if you're considering a production PWA.

```
https://m.phillydevshop.com/apples-refusal-to-support-progressive-web-apps-is-
a-serious-detriment-to-future-of-the-web-e81b2be29676
```

# Tools

Hopefully, you'll be building (many) more Progressive Web Apps in the future. The following tools will make that process easier and faster.

# Workbox

Workbox is "a collection of JavaScript libraries for Progressive Web Apps." More specifically, it "makes it easy to create optimal service worker code" and maintain your caches in the most efficient way. It's easy to integrate into Webpack. Unfortunately, the documentation is not great and customization can be difficult.

Still, Workbox holds great promise as a way to automate aspects of development and hide away complexity that may intimidate new developers. The challenge will be not replacing that complexity with more complexity.

```
https://github.com/GoogleChrome/workbox
```

# Sw-precache

A subset of Workbox, sw-precache is worth discussing on its own. It can be used to automatically generate a service worker to pre-cache your app's assets. All you have to do is incorporate it into your build process (there's a Webpack plugin) and register the resulting service worker.

https://github.com/GoogleChrome/sw-precache

# Sw-toolbox

Not for beginners! Rather than a generation tool, such as the preceding one, sw-toolbox is a collection of helper methods. To add to the confusion, there's also Workbox by the Google Chrome team, which takes a more modular approach. My advice to you is to get comfortable interacting with service workers directly and then, if you have a specific problem that can be streamlined by one of these tools, go ahead and adopt it. However, don't go looking for a tool that solves a problem you don't yet have, but like I said, it's exciting to see tools emerge to help manage the complexity.

https://github.com/GoogleChrome/sw-toolbox

# Offline-plugin

Another plugin to make your app offline-capable. This one uses service workers, but falls back to the AppCache API for better support. Implemention looks simple and straightforward.

https://github.com/NekR/offline-plugin

# Manifest-json

A tool to automatically generate a web app manifest from your command line. I mean, I thought my chapter on manifests was pretty good, but if you prefer a question-and-answer approach, that's fine too, I guess.

Joking aside, this tool may come in handy as Web App Manifests evolve and take on more properties.

https://www.npmjs.com/package/manifest-json

## Serviceworker-rails

Have a Ruby on Rails project? Want your asset pipeline to use a service worker to cache assets? Use this gem. The documentation is an interesting overview on how Rails handles caching and the challenges of implementing a service worker approach.
`https://github.com/rossta/serviceworker-rails`

## Sw-offline-google-analytics

Part of the aforementioned Workbox, but with a specific use for Google Analytics with an offline-capable app. Use this package to send offline requests to Google Analytics as soon as a connection becomes available.
`https://www.npmjs.com/package/sw-offline-google-analytics`

## Dynamic Service Workers (DSW)

Configure your service worker with a JSON file; it's a very interesting approach to service workers, with support for key features such as push notifications (though only with Google Cloud Messaging).
`https://github.com/naschq/dsw`

## UpUp

Add two scripts to your site and have it work offline. UpUp is a beautiful implementation of service worker technology for simple use cases. It's not intended for advanced users, of course, but a great way to introduce service worker technology for everyone.
`https://www.talater.com/upup/`

## Generator-pwa

Generate a Progressive Web App file structure from your command line! This is still a work in progress.
`https://github.com/hemanth/generator-pwa`

# Progressive-webapp-config

Another boilerplate from (you guessed it) Addy Osmani. If you're ever building a non-React PWA, refer to this for project structure.

`https://github.com/PolymerLabs/progressive-webapp-config`

# Stretch goals

Chatastrophe is up and running, but it's still quite basic. We'll now discuss a few challenges, which you should choose to accept, to stretch your skills and improve our app.

# Switch to Preact

Preact is a 3 KB version of the React library. It has a similar API and functionality, without the bulk. Using it instead of React will improve our app's performance. If you do go down this route, look into Webpack aliases as a way of streamlining the conversion.

`https://github.com/developit/preact`

# Show online status

Tell other users when another user is online. The UI is up to you.

# Show when typing

A common feature in chat rooms, it is used to give your users an indication that someone else is typing. With Chatastrophe, the challenge will be representing multiple users typing at once.

# Include file upload

People want to share with their friends (probably memes). Give them a way to do so with a file uploading system.

# Create chat rooms

Your friend had a vision of a truly global chat room; that vision was crap. Let's go ahead and make Chatastrophe much more useable by allowing user-created chat rooms. Is there a way to allow the user to navigate between rooms and read messages even while offline?

# Interactive without React

One of the issues holding back our performance was needing React to boot up before showing the user an interactive site. What if we gave them a purely HTML interactive shell, and then swapped in the React version when it loaded? The challenge here will be avoiding overwriting user input, but you can win some huge performance points.

# Building your own backend

We relied on Firebase for this tutorial in order to keep the attention focused on the frontend, on the React development. However, there's a huge learning opportunity in designing your own backend API for Chatastrophe. The biggest benefit is the possibility of server rendering the pages for extra performance.

# Closing words

Programming is difficult. Learning is difficult. Programming in experimental technologies while learning entirely new concepts is especially difficult. If you completed the tutorial in this book--or even only certain sections of it--you should be proud of the accomplishment.

I sincerely hope what you learned here will be useful for you in your careers. This book has been an exciting journey for me as well. When I started, I was excited about the world of Progressive Web Apps, but by no means an expert. Now, having dived deep into the progressive web, I'm more excited than ever about the possibilities. I hope you share the same feeling.

If you ever want to get in touch, I would love to hear from you--feedback, criticism, questions, or simply conversation. You can find me on Twitter with the handle `@scottdomes`, on LinkedIn, on Medium as `@scottdomes` again, or on my site, `http://scottdomes.com`, where I publish web development tutorials on a wide variety of topics.

# Summary

I hope the mentioned resources will be helpful in continuing your PWA journey. PWAs are an exciting corner of web development that is moving fast; keeping an eye on the preceding authors and creators will help you keep up with the pace of change.

We covered a lot of ground in this book: from nothing to a React app and from a React app to a Progressive Web App. We built an entire application from the ground up and deployed it so that the world could see it. We also made it fast and responsive and able to handle all types of connections.

I hope you're proud of the final application and I hope this book has been useful to you. Good luck with all your PWAs in the future and let's keep progressing the web.

# Index